THE
LITTLE
RED COAT

IRELAND 1927:
THE CAMROSS DROWNINGS

Love and Remembrance

ço

DR. KEVIN FLYNN

ço

Project Manager — Deirdré A. Flynn
Cover photograph of Camross River — credit: Sean M. Flynn
Cover creative and production — credit: Kevin N. Flynn

Photograph page 9 — *credit: Author's Collection*

ISBN-13: 978-1723279942
ISBN-10: 1723279943

Printed by CreateSpace.

࿐

All royalties from the sale of this book will be donated to the
Ailbe C. Flynn LLB, '97 Memorial Scholarship at the Faculty of Law,
Western University, London, Ontario, Canada.

This scholarship was established in memory of my son
Ailbe, 1971 – 2005, through the generous contributions of his family
and friends to Western University, formerly Foundation Western,
in honour of his specialty in Intellectual Property.

࿐

KEVIN FLYNN
KEVINFLYNN3N@HOTMAIL.COM

CONTENTS

৶

☙

DEDICATION

For Mammy and Daddy.

❧

'Beside yon straggling fence that skirts the way,
With blossomed furze unprofitably gay,
There, in his noisy mansion, skill'd to rule,
The village Master taught his little school.'

Oliver Goldsmith — Irish novelist, playwright & poet

'Two less on earth, two more in Heaven,
Gone from our sight yet dear to our love,
The link that unites us is hidden, not riven,
Secured in the hand of our Saviour above.'

Mammy's Prayer Card for Philomena and Maureen Flynn

FOREWORD

KIERAN T. FLYNN

❧

It is my lot to write some words of wisdom about the revised edition of *The Little Red Coat* because I am the elder brother of the author. I am a lawyer in a Country Law Practice in Tipperary Town, since 1954.

Mammy and Daddy left Camross and moved to Tipperary where my brother Sean was born in early 1928, then my brother Paddy in 1929 and I arrived in 1930.

As it happens, I was the first of the Flynns to discover what had transpired in 1927. —How? I was of a curious disposition at 14 years of age, and when my parents were out of the house, I went in under their large bed and brought out a box. Inside, I found hanks of children's hair, hair ribbons and various bits and pieces. There were also newspaper cuttings revealing the family secret, which I never disclosed to my brothers and sisters or of course, to my parents.

What a surprise, therefore, it was for me to become aware of Kevin's odyssey, that led to his discovery in the National Archives of the documented evidence, exhibits and transcripts of the trial some seventy years later.

Of course, *The Little Red Coat* expanded my knowledge of these tragic events. I am full of admiration of the resoluteness of the wonderful research by my brother, Kevin. The wonderful tale now told by him is worthy of the best tales told by the *Seanachaí* (pronounced shan-a-kee), who travelled from one rural parish to another and called to a *Chuarteach* (koor-t-yock) house, a house of welcome, where half the parish would assemble for late evening fireside stories. There would be music and dancing and singing, and even a little courting.

The highlight of the evening was the resumption of the unfinished story by the Seanachaí, which was told to a riveted audience for several hours, but never finished. All were purposely left in suspense at that night's conclusion, to whet their appetite for the next gathering.

I consider that Kevin's recounting is as good, if not better, than any Seanachaí tale I ever heard. When I was in my teens I stayed all summer in the Chuarteach house of my Uncle Jack, my mother's brother. I was sent to his house each summer to get me out of the way.

Despite my deviously acquired previous knowledge of those awful days, I have read *The Little Red Coat* with avid interest in each successive detail. The times that were in it are so well and so awfully portrayed.

This is a compelling read.

Congratulations.

Kieran T. Flynn

Family Photo – early 1927
Statia holding Michael, Patty, Eilis, Maureen, Michael, Philomena (at back)
— *credit: Author's Collection*

PREFACE

࿊

At the National Archives in Dublin in September 1997, my cousin, Elizabeth (Lily) and I received a large brown paper parcel containing all the Criminal Court trial documents for County (Co.) Laois for 1928. We opened it up and on top was the *Book of Photographs* prepared for the Court by the Technical Branch of *An Garda Síochána*, Guardians of the Peace. While I was documenting the list of contents, Lily was perusing the other envelopes. Suddenly she exclaimed:

"Kevin, you will not believe what we have here!"
"What?"
"Look."

Out of a brown envelope she had taken the little red woolen coat worn by Philomena when she was drowned.

Apart from the creases, it was perfectly preserved, showing some dark stains on the sleeves. It was obviously hand stitched, undoubtedly by Mammy. This was the most emotional experience of *The Little Red Coat* project.

After obtaining special permission to photograph it, we returned it to the envelope where it had lain for almost seventy years.

࿊

INTRODUCTION

DR. KEVIN FLYNN

∽

This account of the drownings of my sisters, Philomena and Maureen Flynn in 1927, is presented, not in form of a novel, but as a historical documentary of events based on factual evidence.

It is not possible to describe the emotion of the events. No attempt has been made to dramatize the story beyond the facts. The impact on the people involved can only be imagined. Information is taken directly from depositions, court records and newspaper reports and interviews with people who were connected, directly or indirectly, with those events. Direct quotations are based almost entirely on statements made in depositions and are used in order to make the document more readable. Language of the 1920s may include references or words from witness statements that might not be common today but are included to preserve what was used at the time.

I have drawn on my experience of thirty years as a local Investigating and Inquest Coroner for the Province of Ontario in approaching the project. Nonetheless, it was not always easy to remain objective when children die. Investigation of violent death has changed a lot since 1927 and credit has to go to the *Gardaí Síochána*, Guardians of the Peace, who looked into the Camross drownings without the modern forensic technology we have today.

There is much repetition. There are several reasons for this. Firstly, since the book was intended for the Flynn family, and immediate relatives, and because I believe that all should have access to the same information which I was privileged to see, I have included as much of it as possible without losing continuity. Secondly, without seeing either the scene of the crimes, or the model of the house (missing from the Trial Archives) used at the trial of Mary Cole, it takes some repetition for the reader in order to maintain orientation.

The telling of this story would have been impossible without the help of many people. The support of my siblings, Patty, Paddy, Kieran, Brendan and Ailbe, surviving members of the Flynn family during my year of research, was the first prerequisite. The fact that this revised edition is ninety years since the events described, does not lessen the need which I felt we all had, to bring Philomena and Maureen into the Flynn family. Our children likewise want to know.

Since I first asked for help from my brother Kieran, I have received help without question, and on behalf of the Flynns I thank most sincerely the unselfish contribution by our Flynn cousin Lily and her husband Paddy MacRory. Their neighbour in Dublin, Paddy Nolan, formerly of *The Irish Times* took up the challenge and found the newspaper clippings and the *Judge's Charge to the Jury*. I greatly appreciate the assistance of the staff of the National Archives in providing access to the file of the trial of Mary Cole and photocopying parts of it. Special permission was given to photograph the little red coat worn by Philomena, which appears on the book's front cover. The coat remains in the National Archives.

Others, who prefer to remain anonymous, were instrumental in providing tangible contact with the past and their information was vital in order to complete the story. There was a point during the visit to Camross with Lily and Paddy when I felt that we were being guided by "someone up there". I said to Lily, "God knows, there are enough of us up *there*".

For this new edition, I am deeply indebted to my children, Deirdré and her husband Rob, Sean, Kevin and my late son Ailbe whose gift enabled valuable recordings during research. This revision would not have been possible without their help.

My former office assistant, Barbara, helped with transcribing the lengthy *Judge's Charge to the Jury* and also scanned many of the images. My friend, Denys Horgan, a Dubliner, at the University of California at San Diego helped with editing of the first edition. A mutual friend, a son of Superintendent James Hunt who was a key investigator named John, and John's daughter Eileen, became acquaintances of mine in Canada. Denys' father, Detective Sergeant (retired) Michael Horgan, entered the story many years ago as a Crime Scene Officer.

Special thanks are also due to Gerard Dooley, a historian and native of Camross. He is the author of *Camross, Her People, Their Story* published in 2015. Ger has given his permission for the reproduction of segments of his book research and illustrations.

Martin Delaney, Parish Priest in Rathdowney helped to close some loops in the story of *The Little Red Coat*, with his generous time and advice.

In the event that this manuscript is seen by relatives of Mary Cole, it should be said that there is no lingering rancour on the part of the Flynn family for the tragedies of 1927. We pray for all who suffered in both families in the hope that children everywhere be kept safe from harm.

Finally, this book is dedicated to the memory of our parents Anastatia (Statia) and Michael Flynn. We, who have so much to thank them for, will never know the anguish and pain suffered by them in those summer months of 1927 and during the trial of Mary Cole in March 1928. Each of us knows, however, the sacrifices made by them to get us on our way.

We who grew up with little facts surrounding the tragedy owe a huge debt to our parents who moved on from their loss. Without exception, all ten of us inherited some of the tenacity, and endurance exemplified in their lives. Their own trial can only be imagined after reading their depositions and accounts of their evidence at the trial of Mary Cole.

Their pain cannot be measured.

Their faith helped them to remain resolute and to continue their lives and their dedication to their children and their vocation.

Those were exceptional times, and they were exceptional people. We thank you Mammy and Daddy.

❧

May God bless them,
and the children who came under their care
at home and school.

Ar dheis Dé go raibh a n-anamach

❧

MAP OF IRELAND SHOWING
COUNTIES TIPPERARY AND LAOIS

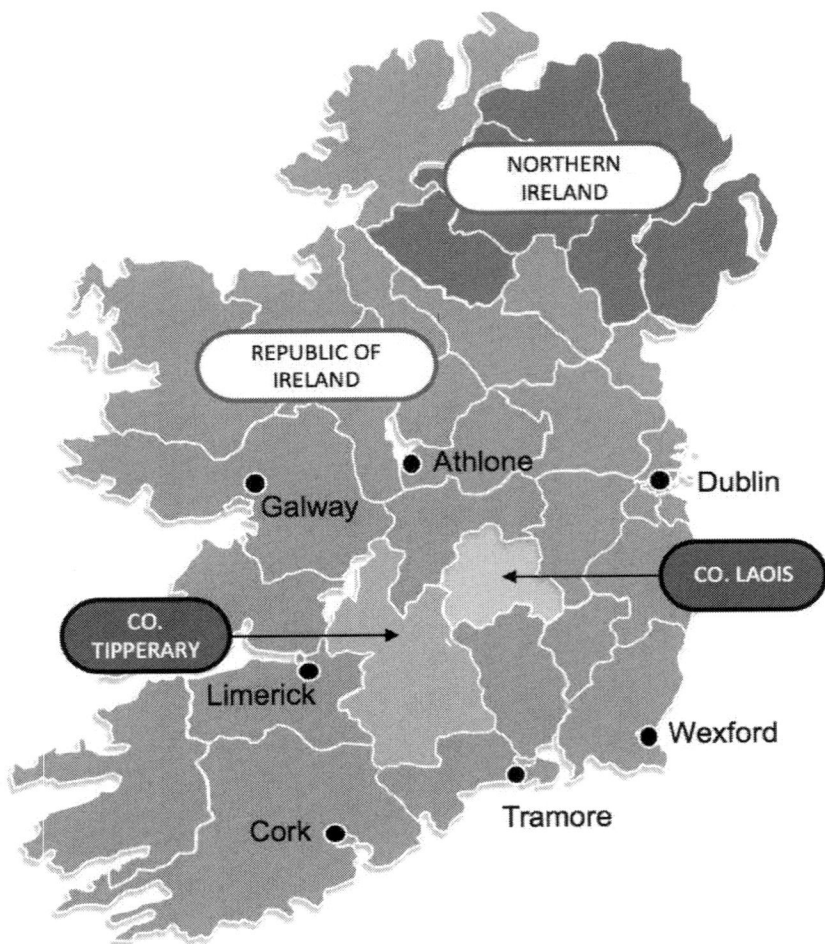

NORTHERN
IRELAND

REPUBLIC OF
IRELAND

Athlone

Galway

Dublin

CO. LAOIS

CO.
TIPPERARY

Limerick

Wexford

Cork

Tramore

MAIN TOWNS OF COUNTY LAOIS

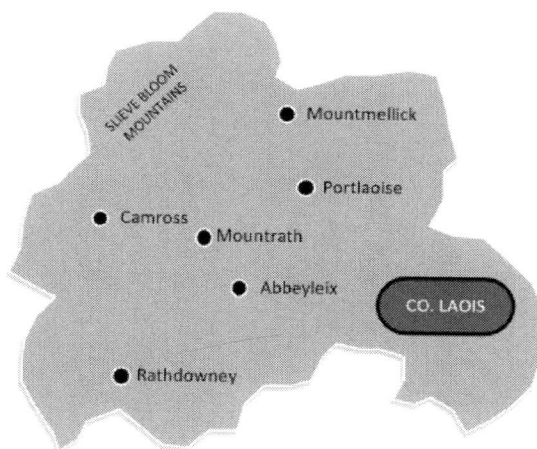

ORDNANCE MAP OF CAMROSS

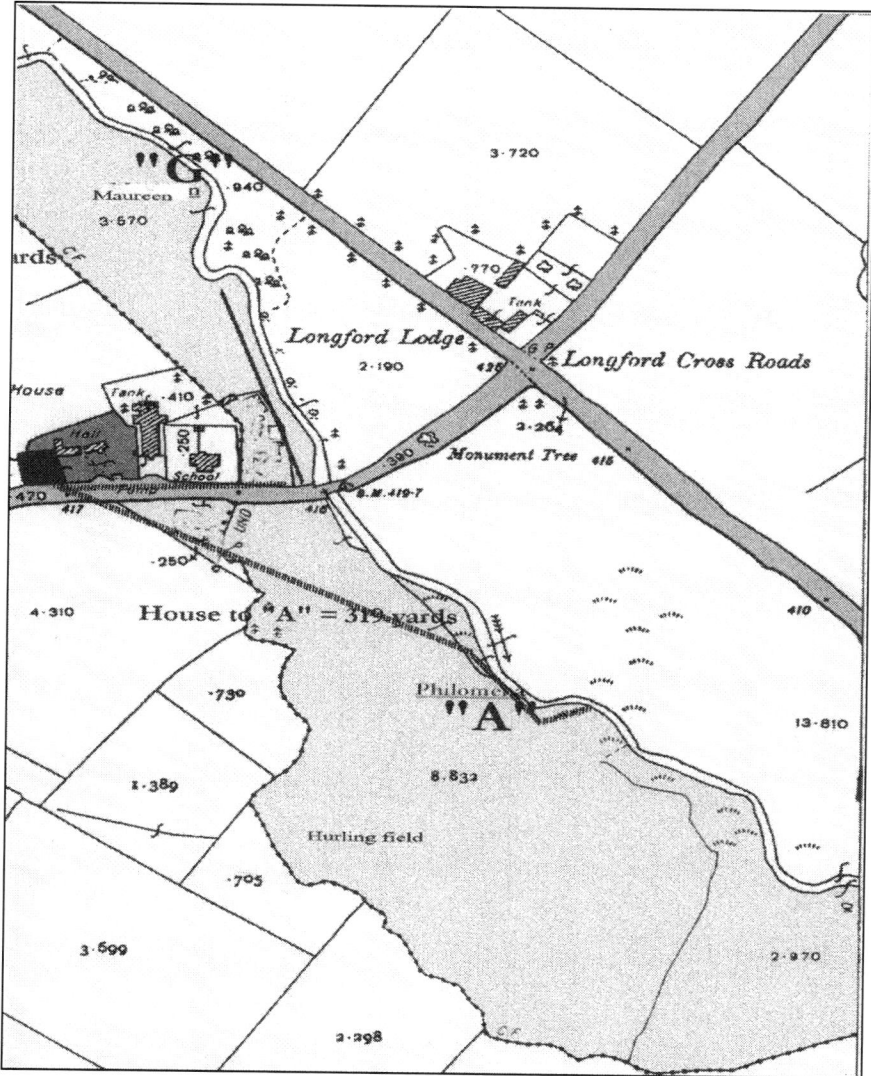

Prepared by the Technical Branch of the *Gardaí Síochána*
— source: *Trial Evidence 1928*

FLYNN FAMILY HEADSTONE
RATHDOWNEY, CO. LAOIS

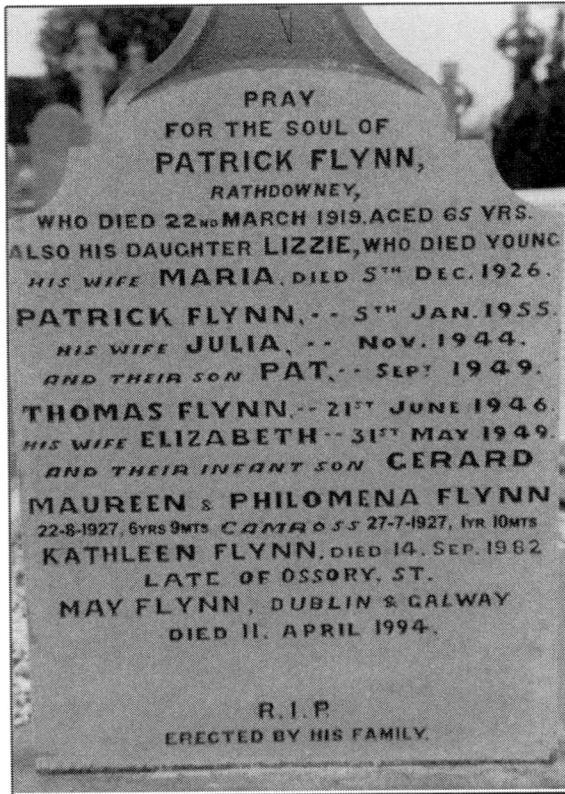

Maureen and Philomena's ages and dates of death
were added with love and remembrance in 1998.
— *credit: Author's Collection*

CHAPTER ONE

SEPTEMBER 26, 1997

❧

MAUREEN & PHILOMENA FLYNN
CAMROSS

On the headstone of my grandfather's grave in Rathdowney Cemetery, in County Leix, *Laois*, the children's names were engraved sometime between 1949 and 1982. Without their ages and dates of death, the passerby would never know that there was a sad and tragic story behind the simple inscription.

At twelve o'clock noon on this Friday, a beautiful sunny Irish day, Paddy MacRory drove us across the narrow bridge over the Camross River and entered the little village at the edge of Slieve Bloom Environmental Park. A wide street wound gently upwards past a one storey red brick school to the right, a thatched cottage of stone, now a heritage centre, an ivy-covered two storey house up a short lane and past St. Cavan's Church and the cemetery. We reached the end of the little village after a few more houses and turned around to get our bearings.

On Wednesday at the National Archives in Dublin, Paddy, my cousin Lily (a Rathdowney Flynn) and I had seen the photographs shown at the trial of Mary Cole in 1928. The sepia-tinted photographs, fading at the edges, told us that the Master's House should be on our left and the old school should be between the house and the river. Lily and Paddy had not been here for over forty years and I knew Camross by name only. It was a one street community and appeared deserted.

"Paddy, pull over here," said Lily from the back seat, "there's an elderly lady coming out of that house and we should ask her where the old school was situated." Lily had been told already that the school-master's house was torn down in 1960. I rolled down the front passenger window as the car came to a stop.

"Excuse me Ma'am, would you happen to know where the old National School used to be?" The kindly, white-haired lady, short and bespectacled, was coming out of a gate beside the car and appeared only too willing to help.

"Certainly," she said, "it was where the new school is now. You can see it from here down the road there on the left." Lily leaned over from the back seat: "This is Doctor Kevin Flynn from Canada. Kevin's father and mother taught at the old school seventy years ago," she said.

"Oh, I remember Mr. and Mrs. Flynn well." She leaned closer to the car. "Sure I was taught by Mrs. Flynn." This immediately stirred our interest.

"So you're one of the Flynns?"

"I am indeed. I was born in Tipperary, long after my parents left Camross. I'm a doctor in Ontario. You are from around here, are you?"

"Yes I am."

"Kevin is looking into the deaths of his two sisters, Philomena and Maureen."

"Oh, sure I went to school with your sisters Maureen and Eilis. Wasn't it a terrible tragedy?"

"Do you have time to talk to us?" We quickly got out of the car.

"Certainly," she said, "I only come here now and then. I live in Abbeyleix now."

She told us she had been teaching abroad with cousins of ours who were regular visitors to Tipperary whenever they were home on holidays and through them she knew of Father Michael, my brother, a Holy Ghost missionary in The Gambia, West Africa.

I checked the little tape recorder my son Ailbe had given me for my sixty-fifth birthday five days before in Canada. I grabbed my notepad and held the tape recorder flat against it. I wanted this conversation to run smoothly but I was afraid I might not recall later what I was about to hear. My head was still reeling with the discoveries of the past few days: the photographs, depositions, Court documents, the *Judge's Charge*, the hand-written verdict of the twelve-man Jury, and sentence by the Court. But most poignant was the discovery of Philomena's little red coat, handmade by our mother.

Our new friend did not remember Philomena but she remembered Maureen as a "happy, lively girl with dark red hair, who used to skip down the road." Maureen, Eilis and Patty were in school together.

Our original plan was to drive to Camross on the following Sunday on our way to Tipperary. This short visit was planned months ago in Canada.

I arrived, as planned, in Dublin on Tuesday, spent Wednesday at the National Archives with Lily, searching old files at *The Irish Times*, the Registry of Births, Deaths and Marriages and The National Library. Thursday was the fortieth Class Reunion of Medical Graduates at University College Dublin (U.C.D.). However, on Friday, we decided to drive to Tipperary via Rathdowney to visit the cemetery where Philomena and Maureen are buried.

Had we not changed our plans, and visited Camross on Sunday instead of this day, we would never have made this connection to the past. We would have been lost in the village where the murder by drowning of two of the school-master's children is not spoken of but where there are still people who remember. If we had not stopped at Rathdowney Cemetery we would not have arrived in Camross at this precise moment.

We would not have seen where the children were actually drowned or retraced the steps taken by the searchers, including Mammy and Daddy.

We would have missed seeing the roll books of the National School with the neatly inscribed names of the boys and girls, *buachailí agus cailíní*, made by the hand of *Stáis Bean Ní Floinn*—my mother—Statia Flynn.

We would not have seen where the attendance of Maureen—*Mairín Ní Floinn* (R.I.P.), was struck off by a line drawn by her own mother through the school record on August 27, 1927, a few days after her death.

NATIONAL SCHOOL ROLL BOOK
CAMROSS 1927

Maureen's name crossed out by her own mother.
— *credit: Author's Collection*

CHAPTER TWO

DISCOVERY

❧

My interest began with a very badly water stained certificate of *Consecration of the Family to the Sacred Heart* that I had picked up at our old family home in Tipperary the previous year. Later I realised that part of the staining was caused by smoke and water in a fire. "If you see anything from the old home you like take it with you," my nephew Anthony Flynn had told me.

"Oh I remember this. I had to kneel before it every evening for years while we said the family Rosary. Parts of it were engraved in my brain."

Growing up in Tipperary, I was the seventh of the ten children whose names were inscribed on the certificate in my father's unmistakable teacher's hand. After Michael J. Flynn and Statia Flynn came Eilis, Patricia, Michael, Sean, Patrick, Kieran, Kevin, Brendan, Colm and Ailbe.

The daily routine after supper was the Rosary and then homework, and if you were old enough you could then go wherever you had plans for the rest of the evening. Woe betide anyone who did not wait for the Rosary. Keeping track of the Hail Marys while your mind was somewhere else was a constant challenge.

"One of ten." How many times had I answered thus whenever I was asked how many children were in my family? "Eight boys and two girls."

Later, after leaving home, I might add "Actually my parents had two children before the ten but they were drowned one day by a crazy maid." This was the extent of my information and I think I only found out that much, like sex, by osmosis. One acquired the knowledge. The true story would never be told because just as the mere fact of two drownings was discovered, unofficially we all knew that we must not bring up the subject at home. I once told the story of a drowned child who was brought into Casualty at Jervis Street Hospital where I trained and I saw eyebrows raised on the faces of older siblings. I knew their names were Philomena and Maureen after I discovered a transcript with some photographs one day when I was rooting around some drawers but I had no time to learn more. The transcript disappeared after that.

So, until a year ago, the extent of my knowledge, erroneous as it turned out, was only that two sisters, Philomena and Maureen, had been drowned in Camross, both at the same time; that they were very close in age; that the maid was sent to an asylum and there were rumours that the deaths were punishment for Daddy's ploughing through a fairy rath![1] I did not buy the superstition in that last part but I settled for the rest and was content to let the world know that I was one of ten, but that actually my mother had given birth to twelve children. The framed certificate of *Consecration* was put away in my basement in Port Credit, Ontario pending 'someday' when I would reframe it. Then I decided to renovate my basement in the early months of 1997, which meant that I had to empty it of accumulated junk. I accidentally kicked and broke the glass of the framed certificate.

"Shit!" I said to no one in particular, "Now I have to do something about this." So I dismantled the frame and lo and behold three other certificates lay underneath!

The earliest was undated but after Michael Flynn and Statia Flynn, the names of Maureen and Elizabeth were inscribed on it and it was signed John Ryan, P.P. The next listed Maureen, Eilis, Patricia, Michael and one unrelated name of Katherine Murray. This certificate was dated 4th March 1924, and under Maureen's name was the date 22nd August 1927 R.I.P. and the date the change was made was 31st August 1927. It was signed William Walsh P.P.

The third certificate dated 2nd April 1928 listed Eilis, Patricia, Michael, Sean, Katherine Murray and Katie Tobin. and was signed John McGrath, P.P. Tipperary.

---

[1] Thousands of raths, also called fairy circles or *lisheens*, exist in rural Ireland. Some are the foundations of circular houses or burial grounds of chieftains from pre-Christian era. They are treated as semi-sacred places not to be disturbed or destroyed for fear of harm or bad luck to the offender or family. They may also have been used as burial grounds for stillborn or unbaptized/unregistered babies.

Now at last I knew that in 1927, Maureen, the eldest child, died on August 22nd, 1927. But where did Philomena fit in, and who was Katherine Murray? The answer appeared to be that the names of Philomena and Michael had not been added before the double tragedy and that following Maureen's death the family was re-consecrated, with her death being recorded and Michael's name added. It appears that only the names of living children were listed.

By the end of 1927, the Flynns had settled into Tipperary, before the trial of Mary Cole. Sean was born on January 2nd but now the name of Katie Tobin was added to the list.

With these questions, I took copies of the certificates with me to Tipperary in April 1997 knowing that I would be seeing the surviving members of my family, Patty, Paddy, Kieran, Brendan and Ailbe, at the wedding of Kieran's son Ian. No one was able to identify Katherine Murray or Katie Tobin but I discovered that Mammy's sister, Aunt Kit, the last of the Fogartys, who died in 1996, had left some newspaper clippings[1] of the trial of Mary Cole. At my request, copies were sent on to me in Canada and when I read them my eyes were opened.

Katherine (Kate) Murray proved to be the housekeeper hired after Philomena's death and Katie Tobin replaced Mary Cole when the latter's employment as maid ended on August 31st, 1927. I discovered Katie's name had been in the school roll before she was hired. Katherine and Katie moved with the Flynns to Tipperary before the trial.

For the first time I discovered that the deaths did not occur on the same day; that Philomena was one year and ten months old when she died on July 27th 1927, and Maureen, six years and nine months of age died about four weeks later on August 22nd, 1927.

The maid, fifteen-year-old Mary Cole was charged with their murders after she left her employment at the Flynn household. What I was reading was a bizarre story of teenage sexual misbehavior, confrontation with authority, repeated denials, ultimate confession, followed by terrible revenge and retribution by murder and attempted murder by arson.

---

[1] These clippings proved to be from the indictment in Portlaoise in December 1927, when Mary Cole was returned for trial at the Central Criminal Court in Dublin 1928.

I also discovered that far from being "crazy" as we were lead to believe from the misinformation that filtered down in our growing up years, Mary Cole was in fact described during her trial as a mature girl well beyond her age.

I resolved to uncover the story of two lost sisters and to bring them back into the family. From this point on, I was one of twelve. This account will show that Mary Cole had motive, means and opportunity to commit the crimes, the three elements necessary to take the case to trial for murder.

The first *Consecration of the Family to the Sacred Heart*
c. 1921 listing children – Maureen and Elizabeth (Eilis)
— *credit: Author's Collection*

The second *Consecration of the Family to the Sacred Heart*
March 4, 1924 listing children Maureen, Eilis, Patricia, Michael
and Katherine Murray
Revised August 31, 1927 adding R.I.P. to Maureen
— *credit: Author's Collection*

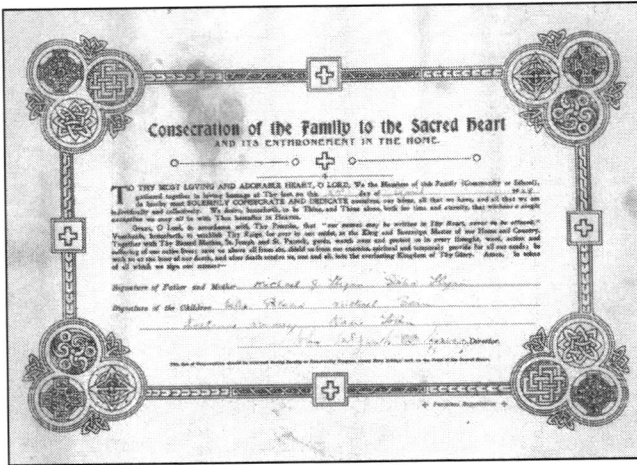

The third *Consecration of the Family to the Sacred Heart*
April 2, 1928 listing children – Eilis, Patricia, Michael, and Sean
Katherine Murray and Katie Tobin
— *credit: Author's Collection*

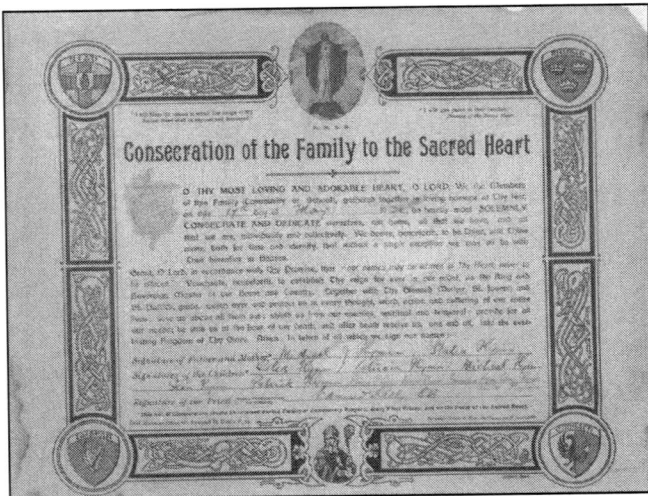

The fourth *Consecration of the Family to the Sacred Heart*
May 17, 1930 listing children – Eilis, Patricia, Michael, Sean,
Patrick, Kieran, Kevin, Brendan, Colm and Ailbe
— *credit: Author's Collection*

CHAPTER THREE

IRELAND IN THE 1920s

To begin to understand the context in which two children met such tragic ends and how a young teenaged girl could be found responsible, one needs to know a little of the social environment that prevailed in Ireland at that time.

On January 11, 1919, two R.I.C. (Royal Irish Constabulary) men were shot dead in County Tipperary in a guerilla action, while transporting explosives. Coincidentally, on the same day the *Sinn Féin* (pronounced shin fayne) government declared independence from Britain. This marked the beginning of the Irish War of Independence but by no means did it end the 'Troubles' that plagued Ireland for years later.

Ireland in the 1920s was still in the throes of civil unrest. England's eight-century grip on Ireland had not been loosened by the Great War of 1914-1918 or by the ill-fated Easter Rising of 1916. The Rising ended with the execution of its leaders and started the atrocities of the Black and Tan years. The creation of the Irish Free State in 1922 marked the end of the War of Independence but the country was not ready for peace.

Continuing agitation and mounting world opinion led to negotiations and signing of the Anglo-Irish Treaty in December 1921, and the creation of the Irish Free State *Saorstát Éireann* in 1922.

The Treaty agreed to the partitioning of six of the nine counties of Ulster in the North of Ireland, heavily populated by non-Catholics and with an important industrial base. This corner of Ireland remained part of the United Kingdom while the other twenty-six counties became independent of direct English rule. However, laws enacted by the Irish Parliament, *Dáil* in Dublin required Royal Assent, represented in Ireland by the Lieutenant Governor, until Declaration of the Republic of Ireland in 1949.

The Dáil was headed by the President of the Executive Council, *Taoiseach*[1], William (W.T.) Cosgrave. Members, *Teachtaí Dála*, or T.D.s, were elected by proportional representation and they had to take an oath of allegiance to HM King George V, his heirs and successors. The anti-Treaty side headed by Éamon de Valera, along with about forty other T.D.s refused to take the oath. De Valera had been head of the titular government that sent Michael Collins to London to negotiate the Treaty. The split between the Old I.R.A. and the elected Government led to civil war in June 1922. The Irish Republican Army opposed the Treaty and 'took to the gun.' An independent Ireland of thirty-two counties was their goal and as far as they were concerned diplomatic negotiation had ended with signing of the Treaty.

The Irish Free State declared the I.R.A. to be an illegal organization and membership in it was a criminal offence punishable by imprisonment. Possession of firearms was punishable by death by firing squad. Civil war was inevitable and the country was torn apart, with brothers fighting brothers and sons fighting fathers, 'Shinners' Sinn Féin against 'Staters' (Irish Free State). One of the early casualties was Collins who was killed in County Cork by an anti-Treaty ambush. Over thirteen thousand Republicans were jailed and the hunger strike became a new weapon in the war.

Retaliation by both sides continued until May 1923 when de Valera, as head of the political wing, ordered Republicans to 'dump arms.' In the following few years some anti-Treaty Republicans continued to carry out random acts of violence, robbery, shootings, while the political wing, Sinn Féin, became the *Fianna Fáil* Party, which succeeded in electing almost half the T.D.s in the 1927 General Election. By signing the Dáil Registry of Oaths and at the same time refusing to take the Oath, de Valera was able to take his seat in the Dáil.

On July 10th, 1927, the Minister for Home Affairs, Kevin O'Higgins was shot dead on his way to Mass by I.R.A. men acting independently. By now the people had seen enough killing and life began to return to normal. Normal in the Ireland of the 1920s was a

---

[1] The term wasn't formally adopted until 1937, but as the President of the Executive Council, Mr. W.T. Cosgrave is generally thought of as the first Taoiseach.

country of mostly small family-owned or tenanted farms—subsistence farming providing food and milk for the usually large families, and maybe some cash crops. Tuberculosis (consumption or T.B.), was prevalent, spread through milk from infected cows, inadequate sanitation and crowded homes without electricity; and there was no cure for T.B.. Public housing was scarce and unemployment was high. Opportunities for escape from the drudgery of rural life were few, usually only through higher education, unaffordable for most, or emigration to England for work.

The switch from an English school system to Irish had an immediate impact in the classroom. The preservation of the native Irish language, long identified with the struggle for independence, had been suppressed, and one of the first changes by the Free State Government was the introduction of compulsory Irish in the schools. Children were now obliged to learn Irish as a first language in the first two years at school and then as a second language in all National Schools. An extra ten per cent was added to marks in subjects taken in Irish, an advantage where jobs were usually awarded to those with the highest marks, especially in the Civil Service. Education was compulsory and free up to age fourteen. 'Mitching' from school was often rewarded by being picked up by the truant officer or by corporal punishment either at home or in the school (often by both). School children walked up to five miles to school, rain or shine. Evidence of the switch to the new administration was to be seen in school roll books which now began to list pupils by their Irish names. National School teachers were enthusiastic supporters of Irish as a living and working language. Attempts to force Irish on pupils usually met with cynical resistance at home. Parents and prospective employers were more interested in skills in the three Rs, reading, writing and arithmetic, than proficiency in what many believed to be a dead language. Parents brought up under the British system were less than enthusiastic supporters unless they were also strongly Nationalistic.

In the small two-teacher rural National School girls and boys were taught together: the junior pupils (infants to third or fourth class) by a female teacher *bean-múinteoir* (pronounced ban mooin-tow-ir) and older pupils (up to sixth or seventh class) by a male *múinteoir*, who was usually the Master, a position of authority and in a small village second in importance only to the Parish Priest.

The two-roomed Camross National School, built in 1909, one of hundreds of identical schools in Ireland, with separate entrances for boys and girls, and separate walled-in playgrounds at the rear was the only educational opportunity for children of the area. Heating was by a turf fire and each pupil was expected to bring a sod of turf during the winter months. Advancement to secondary education meant boarding school or a long bicycle ride to one of the large towns with tuition fees. Practically all of these primary schools have now been replaced by modern brick structures built for a centralised co-educational system. Many of them were abandoned, to be used by farmers or fishermen for storage, as school districts were amalgamated and pupils were driven by bus to central schools. Some of the older schools have been converted to private homes, boutiques or restaurants, especially those located in some of the coastal and more scenic parts of rural Ireland.

Camross National School — *source: photograph from Gerard Dooley*

Michael Joseph Flynn was born on October 7, 1892 in Rathdowney, County Leix, (now called *Laois*), the fourth of seven children, to Patrick Flynn and Maria McEvoy.[1] After attending boarding school at Ballyfin, County Laois, he took teacher training at

[1] Tom, Bill, Pat, Michael, Kieran, Elizabeth, Bridget

De La Salle College in Waterford and after graduation, he was appointed Master at Camross National School in 1915 at age 23.

The school curriculum was dictated by the English-controlled Department of Education and did not include the Irish language or Irish history until the War of Independence. Patrick Pearse described the colonial education system as 'mind numbing' designed to stultify rather than draw out the best in children.

In an interview[1] with journalist Teddy Fennelly, Pat Dowling[2] recalled the influence of Mr. Flynn on his vocation and contribution to education in the village of Camross:

"When I went to school in Camross there was nothing about Irish history, that is until the great Patrick Pearse came along, the great Pearse, he changed Ireland. He was a poet, a teacher, a lawyer and a leader in the War of Independence. He was the man who woke up the people and who got them to stand up for themselves. The Irish were the tools of the overlords for hundreds of years and they had been accepting that position until Pearse came along. When Pearse was executed in 1916, the whole of Ireland changed. After Independence, we got a new teacher, a Mr. Flynn from Rathdowney. The old teachers were all servants of the Crown and taught us nothing of Ireland. The only things we learned were about 'the sun never setting on the King's dominions', 'the black hole of Calcutta', and 'the Irish picking tea in India'. My father knew nothing about Irish history, nor did my grandfather nor great grandfather. You could not blame the majority of Irish people then for being simply not interested in the Rising when it came. They were satisfied with the status quo. They didn't realise they were eating the crumbs from the Englishman's table. But Mr. Flynn was different. He was an admirer of Pearse and loved Ireland and knew its history."

Anastatia (Statia) Fogarty was born on April 17, 1894 to John Fogarty and Mary Connolly at Killoran, Moyne, near Thurles, County Tipperary. One of eight children,[3] she was educated at the Presentation Convent School in Thurles, where she became a monitor, a position given to senior students with an interest in

---

[1] Excerpt from *Camross, Her People, Their Story* (2015) written by Gerard Dooley.
[2] Patrick J. Dowling, a student under Michael Flynn emigrated to San Francisco where he was successful as founding director of the San Francisco Irish Centre. He died in 1998.
[3] Mary, Jim, Ellie, Anastatia, Tom, Pat, Kit, John

entering the order. During a vacation in Tramore, County Waterford, she met Michael Flynn. They courted and she went on to Mary Immaculate Teacher Training College in Limerick.

They were married in the Cathedral, Thurles, County Tipperary on December 30, 1919. Witnesses were Michael's brother, Kieran Flynn, and Madeline O'Reilly.

Maureen was born in Thurles on November 25, 1920. Named Mary at birth after both her paternal and maternal grandmothers, the Irish translation was substituted with the resurgence of the Irish language. They lived in Ballyduff before taking up residence in the Master's House, owned by the Parish and situated between the National School and the Parish Priest's house.

After they were married, Statia took the position of Assistant Teacher in Camross, responsible for the junior classes. Eilis was born on November 8, 1921, Patricia on March 15, 1923, Philomena on September 2, 1925 and Michael on September 18, 1926.[1] Childbirth was supervised by the local midwife, in the two storey stone house, with no running water except what was collected in a rain barrel and hand-pumped into the scullery. Electricity had not yet arrived to rural Ireland. The Master's House was set back about ten yards from the road that winds down from a gentle hill towards the Camross River, passing the church, the Parish Priest's house and Phelan's shop.

The Master's House — *source: Trial Evidence 1928*

[1] The next seven children were born in Tipperary: Sean, January 2, 1928; Patrick, May 19, 1929; Kieran, December 19, 1930; Kevin, September 10, 1932; Brendan, January 24, 1935; Columba, February 4, 1937; Ailbe, October 15, 1942

CHAPTER FOUR

SEPTEMBER 1926
MARY COLE IS HIRED

∂

Mary Cole was born on November 13, 1912 to Thomas and Julia Cole (Carrol), in Derrylahan, near Camross. She was the eldest of seven children. Her father was a labourer who had served with the British Infantry in the Dardanelles Campaign in World War I. Mary attended the National School in Camross from 1917 to July 1926. She was a pupil of Statia Flynn and left school in 1926 at the age of thirteen and a half.

In September of that year Statia hired her as a live-in maid. She was a 'big, intelligent strapping girl' who looked older than her age and well able to do the many chores associated with a household of five children, like carrying two buckets of water from the pump at Tynan's across the road.

Mary was a 'maid of all work' which meant doing general house-work: making breakfast, cleaning, washing clothes, going for 'messages', milking, and caring for the children when the parents were not around. She was given strict instructions not to leave the children by themselves whenever the parents were not home. A handyman would help with the heavy work and the older children were expected to help out when able.

Michael was born on September 18, 1926. Therefore, Statia would have returned to teach probably by the end of October. Maureen, aged six, and Eilis, aged five, had already been enrolled at school and Patty, aged three and a half, probably started when Statia returned to teach, which left Mary Cole at home with baby Michael and Philomena, aged eleven months.

Since the house was next door to the school, it was usual for local teachers and pupils to go home at noon for the main meal of the day, usually called 'dinner'. The evening meal in Ireland was then called 'tea' and consisted of a light meal such as soup and sandwich and maybe fruit cake and tea.

It is likely that Mary only had to keep an eye on the two children and would have been instructed to go next door to the school if the need arose.

Michael Flynn, brought up in a farming family, had bought two fields close to the school. One, across the road from the Master's House and the school, known as the Hurling Field, was at the end of the village, bordered on one side by the Camross River. A wooden gate opposite the school, hung from a post by hoop-iron, opened into the field. A rough-hewn gate of poles of wood led from the left side of the road beside the bridge to the second field between the school and the river.

He kept about twenty cattle and one or two milk cows. Income from sale of the cattle supplemented his salary, which while meager, was a lot more than most of the villagers, especially since both were teachers. This allowed them a few extras such as a live-in maid, a motor car and summer holidays at the seaside in Tramore.

The Camross River, with its origin in the Slieve Bloom Mountains, meandered through the village, and under the bridge that led to Longford Cross. Varying in width from eight to twelve feet, it rarely exceeded ten inches in depth in the summer. Gravel shoals created several crossing places and also provided building gravel to local farmers. The river banks were edged with furze, briars and blackberry bushes and deep paths were worn to the water's edge where cattle went to drink or crossed to the other side.

On June 30, 1927, a relative of Mary Cole, came to see Statia Flynn with a complaint that there were rumours in the village about Mary. She had been seen hanging about with a group of older local teenage boys and would meet them when out for messages. The relative heard that Mary spent the previous night with one of the boys in the Master's car in the garage while the family were asleep. Statia took Mary aside and asked her if it was true. Mary swore that it was not true.

"Let me go home to my mother and I'll go and drown myself", she said.

Statia told her she would not let her go home until she was sure if she was innocent or guilty but that if she told the truth she would be a friend to her. Mary then named the boys that had come to her bedroom window and asked her to come out to the yard but she swore that she did not leave her bed.

Statia was pregnant with Sean. She told her husband of the complaint and of her conversation with Mary. He sent for the three boys. He asked them if they had been on the premises and if there had been other boys with them. They admitted that they had been there at the invitation of Mary Cole. They gave the names of the other boys. They said they asked her to go out with them and she said she would go with one if the others left. One boy remained behind after they left, sometime after midnight. Mary denied this and said that she told them to leave or she would tell Mr. Flynn. The boys accused her of lying.

Mary Cole's bedroom — *source: Trial Evidence 1928*

Michael sent Statia for Father Walsh P.P., (Parish Priest). Father Walsh came and indicated that he would have to look into the matter and asked the boys to return the following night at nine o'clock with the others. Michael spoke to the boy involved the next morning and asked him to come to the house that evening.

While Father Walsh, Michael, the four boys and five others who had been named, waited in the parlour, Statia took Mary into the kitchen. She asked her again to tell the truth, for the sake of her little sick sister, before she would have to admit it before the men. Mary then said that it was true.

41

"I did go out but it was his fault," she confessed.

Father Walsh came into the kitchen and Statia told him Mary had admitted that she had spent the night in the car with one of the boys. Michael wanted to send her home to her family.

"Oh, the poor little Magdalen[1]. Keep her and be a mother to her and don't send her home," Father Walsh pleaded. "Keep her for charity sake."

Michael agreed and as far as he was concerned the matter ended.

Mary's mother came to the house on the following Saturday. Statia told her in Mary's presence what had happened and asked her to speak to the girl and to try to find out what had actually taken place.

"I would like you to take her home to her father so he can talk to her," said Statia.

Mrs. Cole promised to come the next day to take Mary home.

She arrived after Mass and three hours later returned with Mary and said that her father never said a word to her, but that he was "giving out all the time" about Mr. and Mrs. Flynn.

Statia told Mrs. Cole and Mary that she had not definitely decided to keep her but that it would depend on her conduct. She asked Mary to return a navy jumper and costume she had given her. "She got giddy when she was given the clothes," Statia told the Court later.

If she did keep her she would deal severely with her. Furthermore, if she decided to dismiss her, she would not give her a recommendation, and she would consider it her duty to tell any new employer about her conduct. She asked her mother not to supply her with clothes and also said she would not allow her to wear a costume and other things she had given her until she showed repentance.

"A little humiliation will be good for her."

After the Rosary that evening, Mary came to Statia on her knees and asked for forgiveness. "You have children of your own," she pleaded. Statia was not going to parley with her about forgiveness.

"Your conduct in the future will be the best proof of your repentance," she told her.

---

[1] In the Bible, Mary Magdalene is referred to as a fallen woman. She stayed with Jesus in his preaching and was present at the foot of the Cross.

For the next two weeks she appeared to be sulking and not cooperating in her work and asking to be sent home. She was being watched and not given any opportunity for company keeping. After a time, she returned to her normal cheerful self. Statia warmed to her and nothing more was said about the incident.

CHAPTER FIVE

JULY 27, 1927
PHILOMENA IS FOUND

જ

On July 27th, a Wednesday, the Rathdowney Agricultural Show was held and Michael Flynn went there after about eleven in the morning. Statia spent the day at school, came home for lunch and returned at about 3:30 p.m.. She set about preparing dinner for herself.

The children were all in the house. Philomena, one year and ten months old climbed up on a chair and into the baby's pram. As the pram started to upset, Statia caught her before she could hit the ground and comforted her in her arms until she fell asleep. She then put her down to sleep in a cot in the kitchen and served dinner to Mary Cole, Maureen, Eilis and Patty before having her own.

She was never to see Philomena alive again.

Pregnant with Sean, Statia went upstairs to rest and slept until just before the Angelus Bell rang at 6:00 o'clock from the Church next door. As she came down to the kitchen, she observed Mary giving a bottle to baby Michael, aged ten months.

"I'll do that" she said taking Michael from her, "while you bring in the cow."

"We need some calf meal," Mary told her. "Couldn't Maureen do that?"

"It would be too heavy for her."

Statia gave her the money for the calf meal and told her to hurry home as Mr. Flynn was expected and Mary would have to get the tea (evening meal). Mary left for Phelan's shop. Two of the children were playing upstairs and one was downstairs but Philomena was nowhere to be seen. About five minutes later Statia heard Mary talking to someone outside the door and thought it must be Philomena. As she came into the house, Statia asked if Phil was with her.

"Didn't I see her at the window upstairs?", said Mary. Statia told her to check the downstairs rooms.

"When did you see her last?"

"She was there a few minutes ago."

Mary was sent to look for her outside the house and then to Tynan's. Statia set off towards Longford Cross, looking into the field on the right side of the road. Seeing no sign of her she returned home expecting her to have been found at one of the neighbouring houses. Mary Cole was in the yard.

"When did you see her last, Mary?", Statia repeated.

"She was there when I brought in the cow," she said, pointing to the door.

Making a mental note that this was the first she heard that Mary had already brought the cow in from the field while she was upstairs resting, Statia sent her across the field to Father Walsh's while she searched the outhouse. She then started back towards Longford Cross, meeting some villagers on the way. Nobody had seen the little girl. She went through the gate into the field across from the school. She went through one field and came back by another, along the river, calling out her name as she went. As she was coming from the river about five yards from where the child's body was later found, she met Mary Cole coming towards her.

"There's no use going any further, Mary. No child would go down there."

They walked quickly towards the house. She told Mary to ask anyone she met to search the field on the other side of the road. Statia met John Tynan, the thirteen-year-old son of her neighbour across the road from the Master's House. John was on his way home from Gleeson's and on hearing that Philomena was missing he went through his father's land and met up with his friend Tommy. They both went into the Hurling Field towards the river.

Statia met John Gorman on the road outside her house. It was now about 7:30 p.m.. She asked him to join in the search and hurried on to Father Healy's house. She asked the priest to ride his bicycle in the opposite direction up towards Marymount Cross and to come back and tell her if he had any tidings of the child.

John Gorman crossed over the bridge and into the field on the right. He walked along the left bank of the river and after about twenty yards he met Mary Cole. She was on the opposite side about sixty yards from him and about thirty yards from the river. She was coming towards him beside a barbed wire fence.

"We're looking for Phil, Johnny. Wouldn't it be awful if she was drowned?"

Mary turned and faced down the river. He asked her if she had searched down the river already but he did not hear her reply. She went down the right side and Gorman continued on the left. She was about fifteen yards ahead and after about a hundred yards she called out excitedly, "the child is here!"

He did not believe her at first until he crossed the river and saw Philomena. She was submerged in water face down, dressed in white, her head towards him. He picked her up and laid her on the bank of the river. He called out to Mary "I think she's dead."

He picked her limp body up and carried her in his arms towards the house, Mary Cole walking behind.

As she was nearing her house, Statia Flynn saw approaching her at a distance coming from the direction of the river a procession of John Gorman, Mary Cole and John Tynan. Gorman was carrying her child.

"Is she all right?" she called out anxiously.

"She's dead, Missus," young Tynan cried out. They went in the house ahead of her and as she entered she saw the body of her youngest daughter on the table in the kitchen. Mary Cole stood quietly behind the body, saying nothing. She had no tears for the child she was hired to mind.

The doctor was sent for from Coolrain, about three miles away. Dr. Kieran Phelan, a House Surgeon from the Meath Hospital in Dublin, was acting as *locum tenens* for Dr. McCarthy, the Dispensary Doctor.

Michael Flynn arrived back from the Rathdowney Show at 10:00 p.m. to find his daughter dead on the kitchen table.

Dr. Phelan arrived at about 11:00 p.m.. He pronounced death and examined the body. He found no external injuries and formed the opinion that she had died of asphyxiation by immersion in water.

The Coroner was notified and the next day an inquest was held. Mr. E.J. Conroy, Coroner for County Leix, heard evidence from Statia Flynn, Mary Cole, John Gorman, John Tynan, Dr. Phelan and the Gardaí.

There was no postmortem examination on the body. The Coroner accepted the medical evidence and returned a verdict of Asphyxia by Immersion in Water on Thursday, July 28, 1927.

On Friday, the day after the inquest, Mary's mother was helping at the house and a conversation took place in Mary's room between Mrs. Cole and Statia. Mrs. Cole wanted to send Mary to a relative in England. Statia told her that Mary would have to work out a month's notice to August 31st. After her mother left, Mary came to Statia and told her she did not want to leave.

"I don't want to go to England," she said, "I'd rather stay with you and I'll try to get my mother to let me stay."

"Isn't it strange for her to say she placed the death of Phil at my own door, and to say that the neighbours did likewise? Wouldn't it be time enough when I'd blame myself for carelessness leading up to the death of the child to throw the blame on me?", said Statia.

"It would be too late then. Don't mind my mother. She has a terrible temper and it's not a bit like her."

After the inquest, it was agreed by Michael and Statia that she should take Maureen, Eilis and Patty to the seaside at Tramore, which was pre-arranged and where they went every summer for holidays.

While she was away, Katherine Murray started as housekeeper on August 6, 1927. Michael remained home with the baby. On August 16th Statia and the children arrived home.

Philomena was found 319 yards from home. Star indicates location.
—*source: Trial Evidence 1928*

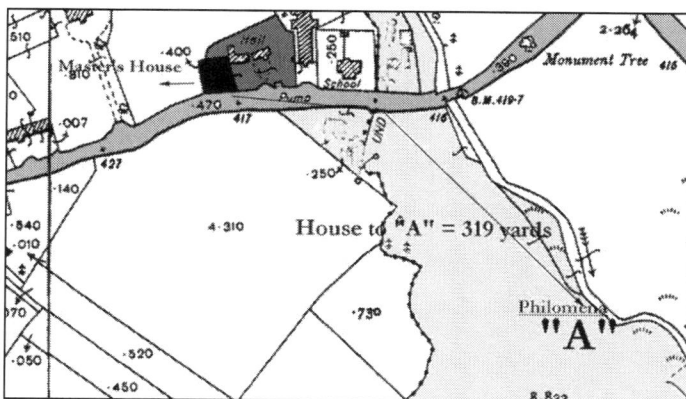

—*source: Trial Evidence 1928*

Philomena Flynn
Camross
Died July 27, 1927
Aged 1 year, 10 months
— *source: Author's Collection*

49

CHAPTER SIX

AUGUST 22, 1927
MAUREEN IS FOUND

છે

On Monday, August 22nd it rained until late in the afternoon. School was still closed for the summer holidays and everybody was home. Michael Flynn was in the parlour reading. Statia was in the kitchen with Katherine Murray and the baby, Michael. Mary washed up after dinner and went to her room with Maureen until 5:00 or 5:30 p.m. Eilis and Patty were playing in the turf shed. Mary and Maureen set about preparing food in the scullery for the calf. Mary came into the kitchen for a kettle of hot water.

At about 5:35 p.m. Maureen returned to the kitchen with the kettle of water and reached across her Mammy to put it on the hob. She went back to rejoin Mary in the scullery.

That was the last time Statia Flynn saw her eldest daughter alive.

About ten minutes later Kate Murray asked for Maureen. Outside in the yard, there was no sign of either Mary Cole or Maureen. Statia thought the two had gone for the cow.

After about twenty minutes, Mary came back alone with the cow. Kate asked her if she knew where Maureen was.

"No" she replied.

Kate told Michael and Statia that Maureen was missing and went to Phelan's shop to look for her. Mary was milking the cow in the cowshed. Michael went out and told her to look for Maureen, first at Father Walsh's, then at Pratt's.

Michael went to the school playground.

He met Mary as she was coming from Pratt's and he sent her up the road. Statia went to where Philomena had been found while Michael searched the opposite side of the river.

He sent Statia home and went to search along the river in the field on the left side of the road.

After about a hundred yards he saw her.

Maureen was found 245 yards from home. Star indicates location.
— *source: Trial Evidence 1928*

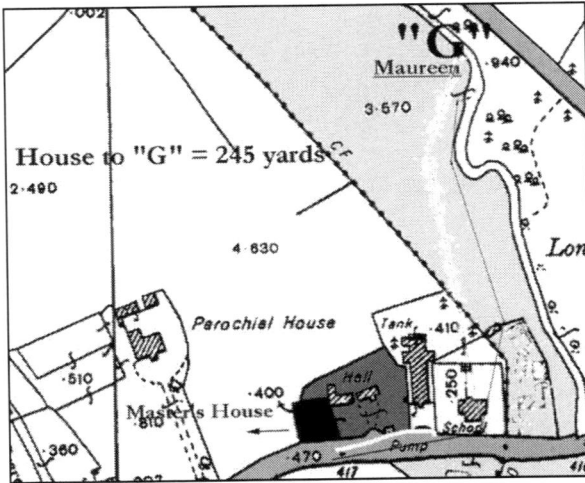

— *source: Trial Evidence 1928*

Maureen Flynn
Camross
Died August 22, 1927
Aged 6 years, 10 months
— *source: Author's Collection*

Thirty yards in front of him his eldest daughter was laying in the river, parallel to the bank where the river was split in two by a gravel island. He hurried towards her through briars and furze to reach her. In the branch of the river nearer to him, about four feet in width, she lay on her right side, head bent forward against the flow of water with her left leg flexed. The face and left side of her body were above the water. She wore neither shoes nor stockings.[1]

Rushing across the shallow water he lifted her out and laid her on the grassy bank. There was froth at her mouth and her body was limp. The left side of her forehead was bruised.

Certain that she was dead, he nevertheless tried to revive her.

In a few minutes he carried her home and laid her on the bed in Mary Cole's room and sent for the doctor.

"Where did you find the cow, Mary?" Michael asked.

"She was at the far end of the field beside the school," she said. Michael knew that twenty or so cattle were in that field. They were free to cross the road from one field to the other under the bridge and the cow usually went with them.

Maureen was afraid to go near the river following the death of her sister. A couple of days ago Michael took the children with him to bring in the cow and left them on the path that runs through the field. As he walked towards the cow Maureen began to cry and he went back and took her with him.

Dr. James McCarthy, the Dispensary Doctor in Coolrain, arrived at the Master's House between 7:30 and 8:00 p.m. Maureen was wrapped in a blanket before the fire in the kitchen. Although she appeared dead, he attempted artificial respiration, usual with drownings.

After a couple of hours, he declared her to be dead. On superficial examination he found a slight bruise on the left side of the forehead but no other marks of violence. Her face was purplish and her eyes and mouth were partly open.

The next morning Superintendent Carmody, from Mountrath, accompanied Michael Flynn and Dr. McCarthy to the river to inspect the spot where she was found.

Dr. McCarthy gave evidence at the inquest on August 23, 1927

---

[1] Typical in 1927 for rural children to walk barefoot in the summer time.

before the Coroner and the verdict returned was Asphyxia and Shock due to Accidental Drowning.

On the day after the inquest, Maureen was laid out in the parlour. She was due to make her First Communion in two weeks with her school class.

Statia had prepared the First Communion class and, as she did every year, she presented each child with white Rosary beads. They recited the Rosary, kneeling around Maureen's body.

Maureen was taken to be buried in the Flynn plot in Rathdowney Cemetery, alongside her little sister Philomena.

CHAPTER SEVEN

AUGUST 25, 1927
THE FIRES BEGIN

☙

On Thursday, August 25th, three days after Maureen's drowning, everybody was in bed by 10:00 p.m. as usual. Statia and Michael and baby Michael slept in the room over the parlour. Kate Murray and Eilis and Patty slept in the room over the kitchen. Mary Cole slept in a room downstairs at the back of the kitchen. At about midnight, Kate awoke to a crackling noise and got out of bed. About half way downstairs she saw the light of flames from the front room. She ran to the bedroom door of Mr. and Mrs. Flynn.

"Get up quickly, the parlour is on fire!"

Michael and Kate ran downstairs. The curtains on the parlour window were burning. Statia hurried to Mary Cole's room.

"Get up, Mary. The house is on fire. Get some water!"

Sparks and flames flew from the casement around the window and the sofa in front of the window was smoldering. Michael took water from the scullery and poured it on the sofa, while Mary filled a pail from the tap. They succeeded in quenching the fire and eventually returned to bed.

Next morning Statia spoke to Mary about the fire.

"I don't want anyone to know about the fire, Mary. There is enough talk going around about us."

After breakfast, Mary helped Statia clean up after the fire and they pasted wallpaper over the burned casement. While doing so Statia found a burned match between the curtain area and the window.

"Could that match have caused the fire, Mary?" she asked.

"If it was the match it would have burned a hole in the floor," Mary said.

The curtains were replaced a few days later on Sunday, August 28th.

On Tuesday, August 30th, the day before Mary's employment was to end, everybody was in bed by 10:00 p.m.. At about 1:00 a.m.

Michael was awakened by a noise from the parlour. He immediately jumped out of bed to find the upstairs corridor full of smoke. He ran downstairs and into the kitchen, calling out for Mary as he went for water. The parlour door was open.

"The smoke was so dense that I could not enter," he told the Court later. "I could see three distinct fires, one at the front window, one at the back window and one on the sideboard at the end. I eventually got into the room and found papers were burning."

"The fire at the back window seemed the worst. Pictures had fallen. The paper around the window and along the wall for about four feet had been burned."

Mary Cole handed him a can of milk to help quench the fire. Statia sent her upstairs to Kate's room to attend to baby Michael who was crying. Michael continued to fight the fire.

Shortly after sending Mary upstairs, he heard a noise of something hitting the corrugated iron roof of her room. He shouted up to her: "Is that noise over your head, Mary?"

"No," she said.

Next morning a hairbrush was found on the roof above Mary Cole's window.

Later there would be talk of ghosts.

CHAPTER EIGHT

AFTER AUGUST 31, 1927
GARDAÍ INVESTIGATE

಄

On Wednesday, August 31st, Mary Cole left her employment at the Flynn's to work for the Murphy family at Rushin House, outside Camross. She was given a little going away gift by Statia Flynn.

Various rumours began to circulate around the area. These ranged from superstitions, *piseógs*[1] (pronounced pish-ogues), to ghosts haunting the Master's House, to insurance claims by Michael Flynn on the deaths of his two children. (There was no insurance on the house or the children). Gardaí investigators continued their inquiries after the inquest, under Chief Superintendent Peter Bracken of Tullamore assisted by Superintendent Dennis Twomey and Superintendent James Hunt. Several people from the village and surrounding areas were interviewed and asked to make statements[2] and Mary Cole was brought to Mountrath Station several times for questioning.

The Flynns moved from Camross before the new school year 1927/1928 for positions in the Tipperary National School and Ballyhurst N.S.. For Michael, he was the new Master at the boys' National School and in nearby Ballyhurst for Statia, a small two-room country school similar in size to Camross. They took with them Katherine Murray and Katie Tobin. Statia was pregnant with Sean who was born in Tipperary in January 1928. Statia would later become Head Mistress at the girls' National School in Tipperary.

SUMMARY OF WITNESS STATEMENTS

Kate Murray described how she became housekeeper at the

---

[1] Regarded as a curse on a neighbour, his crops or cattle. The power of the piseóg lies more in the fear of injury or harm and may be used to explain the unexplainable.
[2] The information which follows is taken from depositions taken at the District Court, and is presented here as background to the statements made by Mary Cole.

Flynns on August 6th while Mrs. Flynn was at Tramore. Mary Cole was then at the house, with baby Michael and Mr. Flynn. Before Mrs. Flynn returned from holidays on August 16th, Mary told her that she "had been greatly wronged by Mr. and Mrs. Flynn by exposing her and taking away her character." She also told her that she "would never forgive Mrs. Flynn for calling in the priest on her." She referred to the costume that Mrs. Flynn had taken from her, but "she did not seem very bitter about that."

Kate told the Garda Superintendent about the fires on the 25th and 30th of August and about finding her hairbrush on the roof of the shed next morning. The brush had been on her dresser before the fire and when asked in Kate's presence by Michael Flynn if she had thrown the brush out the window, Mary began to cry and denied it. Later Kate asked her again if she had thrown it out in her fright she said she did not remember.

After Mary was charged, her solicitor asked Kate if Maureen was fond of Mary. She replied "Maureen was fond of Mary Cole but Mary Cole was not fond of her."

Thomas Brophy, the priest's workman, was cycling to Camross by Longford Cross at about 6:00 p.m. on July 15th. As he passed over the bridge he heard a child crying and dismounted near the Flynn's shed. Looking from whence the crying was coming he saw Philomena in the field three or four yards from the ditch and about one hundred and twenty yards from her house. He realised she could not have gotten into the field on her own and then he saw Mary Cole coming along the road from the same field with the cow. He remained near the child until she drew near and then he told her that Phil was down by the shed and that she should go and bring her home.

Mary Bostick, of Knocknagad, about three miles from Camross, was with her brother Tom in an ass and cart on the way to Phelan's shop in the evening of July 27th. As they passed Longford Cross she did not see anyone in the fields. After about ten minutes in Phelan's they started for home. After they passed the school she saw Mary Cole about nine or ten yards from the gate of the Hurling Field at Longford Cross. She was driving the cow towards the gate. The time was about quarter to six. Mary was alone. The Angelus Bell rang as she arrived at Delour Bridge. By then Mary was back at the house feeding baby Michael as Statia came down from her sleep.

John Hennessy, a farmer from Knocknagad, driving a pony and trap also on his way to Camross with his mother, passed Mary Bostick before Longford Cross. As he reached the Cross about quarter of a mile in front of Mary Bostick, he saw "the Master's maid" in the Hurling Field. She was about "six perches" (33 yards) from the road and she was driving a cow on to the road. He saw a child "dressed in a red costume or cloak" running alongside the maid.

He went on past the school to Phelan's. His mother wanted to see the Parish Priest so he took her to the presbytery. The priest was not at home so he returned to the shop while his mother went down the road. About ten or fifteen minutes later Mary Cole came in for calf meal.

Joseph Delaney was a shop assistant at Phelan's. He knew each of the Flynn children well. He was in the yard of the shop looking out to the road and he remembered seeing Maureen, Eilis and Patty running up the road from their house past the shop at about half past five on July 27th. About seven to ten minutes later he saw John Hennessey and his mother coming up the road. He went into the shop as the Hennessy's were coming and Mary Bostick arrived after a few minutes. He attended to the customers and remembered Mary Cole coming in while Hennessey was there.

At about 5:30 p.m. on the day that Maureen died he saw Mary Cole at the gate to the field near the school. He intended passing by without speaking to her when she said to him 'in a frightened sort of way'. "Good evening Tom." He continued on to Delour Bridge where he saw John Tynan on a bicycle.

Around midnight, August 31st, the night of the second fire, Thomas Brophy was returning late to Father Walsh's house and when at the front door he looked towards Flynn's house and saw a light through the scullery window which faces the priest's house. Next morning at about 7:15 a.m. he met Mary Cole in Flynn's yard.

"Mary, you had a light very late last night, were you reading or what?"

"No. I was writing down cookery notes out of a book," she replied.

Katie Tobin, seventeen-years-old, had been to Camross

School and knew the children well and met Mary Cole several times since the end of August when Mary left to work at the Murphy's at Rushin House.

Mary told her about finding Philomena. She told her that she left Phil playing in the parlour with the other children when she left to bring in the cow. She said that when she came back the child was missing and she went looking for her. She described how she passed the spot where Philomena was found several times and when she found her she told John Gorman.

She told Katie that the day Maureen disappeared she was making up the calf's food and Maureen asked her if she could go with her for the cow.

"No," she told her, "you're too fond of telling tales."

When she got back with the cow, Maureen was missing and she said she was sent to look for her at Phelan's shop, and then to other neighbours including the Gleeson's and the Carey's. She told Katie that she said to Mrs. Carey that Maureen must be drowned.

"Nonsense," she said Mrs. Carey responded, "a child that size getting drowned!"

Mary told Katie about Mrs. Flynn bringing the boys into the parlour and bringing in the priest on her.

"If Mrs. Flynn brought the priest on her twice, she had two inquests in the house afterwards," she told Katie.

Mary Cole also told her about the fire. She said she heard nothing till Mr. Flynn called for something to quench the fire and she handed him the milk. She said after the fire was put out they were all in the kitchen and one of the children was crying upstairs. She said that she went up and just as she entered the room the hairbrush jumped out through the window.

Next morning, she went to Carey's for more milk. She told them "the ghosts drank the milk."

A few days before she was arrested in the middle of November, while discussing the children, Mary Cole told Katie that she had heard that Mr. Flynn had the children insured and that "he got £50 for the first but nothing for the second, it being drowned so soon after the first."

Katie told her she had heard that the Flynns had bought

Burke's farm.

"I heard that too," Mary Cole responded, "and well they could buy it."

Johanna Bergin, who lived in Camross and attended to the doctor, described how she prepared Maureen's body. She said she noticed a mark on her forehead and some fresh blood at the sides of the mouth.

She said Mary Cole came to her house the week after leaving her employment at Flynns.

Mary told her that her sight was bad since the fright she got when the children died. She told Mrs. Bergin about the fires, the curtains and the sofa burning and the pictures falling off the wall. She told her the dressing table and the hairbrush flew out the window while she was downstairs. Mrs. Bergin said the fairies were surely after them [the Flynns].

"I hope not," Mary laughed. "My father and mother can't sleep with me jumping up in my sleep at night."

AUTHOR'S NOTE

❧

The reader of this second edition of *The Little Red Coat* is advised that Mary Cole made two statements to investigating Gardaí.

Statement "A" was made at the Garda Barracks in Mountrath on October 3, 1927 and is included as an addendum for purposes of full disclosure.

For purpose of a complete account and continuity of events, Statement "B" dated November 5, 1927 contains Mary Cole's statement, nine weeks after the end of her employment with the Flynns.

This statement was made at Rushin House, Mountrath where she then worked. It was witnessed by Superintendent James Hunt and Superintendent Dennis Twomey. Her statement includes the events prior to and including the drownings of Philomena and Maureen Flynn and the two arson attempts.

❧

CHAPTER NINE

STATEMENT OF MARY COLE
RUSHIN HOUSE, MOUNTRATH

❧

STATEMENT "B" - NOVEMBER 5, 1927

I will be 15 years of age on the 13th of November. My first employment as domestic servant was with Mr. and Mrs. Flynn, National Teachers, Camross. I entered the service of the latter on the 10th of September 1926. I was then 13 years and 10 months. I had previously gone to school to Mr. and Mrs. Flynn at Camross.

There were four young children in the Flynn family, Maureen, Lizzie, Patricia and Philomena when I entered their employment. Maureen was the oldest and was then six years and Philomena was the youngest and aged about one year. I was only about one week in their employment when Michael was born.

I remained in Flynn's employment until the 31st of August 1927. I had no fault to find with Mr. and Mrs. Flynn as employers: the latter occasionally flew into a temper and checked me when I did anything wrong, but generally she was very nice and good natured.

Sometime last March, Mrs. Flynn accused me of keeping company with boys and threatened to tell my mother if she heard any more complaints. On the 30th of last June Mrs. Flynn accused me of leaving the house at night to meet boys. I denied it. She then called Mr. Flynn and told him I had denied being out at night with boys. Mr. Flynn then accused me of going on several occasions at night after they had gone to bed. I still denied it. He then mentioned the names of several boys that I had gone out to meet and said he would make further inquiries about the matter. After this he left the house and I was upstairs putting the baby (Michael) to sleep when Mrs. Flynn came up and asked me not to leave her employment. (I had threatened to do so earlier in the evening when she accused me of going out with boys) and she further told me that I was not to take the costume she had given me sometime previously as it was still her property. I promised her I would not leave and she then told me to go downstairs and finish the housework.

At about 9 p.m. that night Mr. Flynn returned, bringing with him [three local boys.]

Mr. Flynn asked the three boys in my presence if I ever left the house at night after he had gone to bed. All three admitted coming around the house at late hours but denied that I had left the house to meet them. He then asked them if they were aware of I going to meet any other boy but they denied it. He then asked me if I had gone to meet any of the three boys present or anybody else but I denied it.

He then directed Mrs. Flynn to go for Father Walsh, P.P. who lives close by. While Mrs. Flynn was absent for the priest Mr. Flynn kept accusing me in the presence of the boys of going out late at night and also of meeting boys when going out to the well and on messages. I fainted and when I recovered Father Walsh and Mrs. Flynn were standing in the kitchen. Mr. Flynn then repeated in the presence of Father Walsh what he had heard about me and the boys meeting at night. Mrs. Flynn told Father Walsh that when she questioned me about the matter I had denied it. Father Walsh questioned the boys concerning the allegations made by Mr. and Mrs. Flynn and they admitted being about the house and calling to my bedroom window but denied that I had gone out to them. Both Mr. and Mrs. Flynn had told the priest that they had heard I had gone out to meet a boy ... who was not then present. Mrs. Flynn suggested to the priest that we (the boy and I) should get married.

Mr. Flynn remarked that I was only 14 years and did not understand the seriousness of this conduct, but that the boys should know better as they were old enough. Father Walsh said I was deserving of sympathy on account of my age. Father Walsh questioned me further as to I going out at night and Mrs. Flynn remarked that it was nice conduct I started in their house. Father Walsh and the boys left after this and Mrs. Flynn ordered me to bed. Previous to this I used to sleep in a room on the ground floor behind the kitchen but on this night Mrs. Flynn ordered me to sleep in the children's room upstairs.

On the following morning when Mrs. Flynn was going to school she took all my clothes except what I was wearing and brought them to school with her. The costume that she had previously given me was amongst the clothes she took and I never got this costume back.

About 9 p.m. that night when I was going to bed Mrs. Flynn told me not to go yet and shortly afterwards I heard a lot of voices in the parlour. I recognised Father Walsh's voice. Mrs. Flynn told me that all the boys were inside and that [the boy] was there to say that I left my bedroom at night and went out to meet him. She asked me several times to tell the truth and to give up denying about going out to meet [him]. She said I would be put on my oath and that [the boy] would be there to contradict me if I denied it.

I then told her I left my bedroom on one morning only at 4 a.m. to meet [the boy] and that we were in the motor car in the garage. She replied that she knew all. The boys left shortly afterwards and Mrs. Flynn brought Father Walsh into the kitchen and told him, in my presence, that I had admitted the truth at the eleventh hour. I told the priest that I was ashamed of what I had done and he advised Mrs. Flynn to be a mother to me. After the priest left I was ordered by Mrs. Flynn to sleep in the children's bedroom upstairs.

Subsequent to this night Mrs. Flynn repeatedly taunted me with leaving my bedroom and meeting [the boy] at night and the following day when she was giving me back my clothes she said the priest would be watching me, and on the same evening she sent for my mother and complained about my conduct. She told my mother I would not be allowed to go home unless accompanied by my mother and returning. Whenever I would not do my work satisfactorily she would say that my mind was on boys and not on my work. I heard her tell my mother that she would not be sorry (my mother) taking the stick and beating me and she ordered my mother to tell my father.

On Sunday the 3rd of July 1927 my mother brought me home and returned with me that evening. Mrs. Flynn took her into the parlour and I did not hear what conversation passed between them, but when my mother was leaving the same evening I heard Mrs. Flynn say to her, "I am sorry for giving you the trouble of bringing her home today when her father did not say anything to her". She said to me in my mother's presence that she would forgive me after some time if I changed my conduct and gave up going out with boys and she remarked to my mother that she would be very displeased if she (my mother) bought me any clothes. Mrs. Flynn ordered me to bring the water and to have the cow milked and the calf fed before the boys would gather in the roads in the evening and that I was not to leave the house afterwards.

I should have said that on the first evening, 30th of June 1927, Mrs. Flynn accused me of going out with boys. She said, 'You will be married young like your mother and have 9 or 10 children before you are thirty years of age'. My father has heart disease and Mrs. Flynn on that evening also said, 'Wouldn't your mother be in a nice state if he (my father) died suddenly and you to arrive home with a child in your arms'. I did not know at the time what Mrs. Flynn meant by the latter remark, but when my mother questioned me on Sunday the 3rd of July 1927 as to what [he] done to me, I understood.

Except for occasional remarks by Mrs. Flynn when I did not do my work satisfactorily that it was boys I was thinking of there was no further reference to my conduct afterward.

I remember the 27ᵗʰ day of July 1927. Mr. Flynn went to the Rathdowney Show on that day and Mrs. Flynn returned from school at 3:30 p.m. (old time). The children, Maureen, Lizzie and Patricia (who was also at school) returned before their mother. Philomena and the baby, Michael, were in the house when Mrs. Flynn returned. I prepared the dinner for Mrs. Flynn and the children and while I was preparing dinner Philomena fell asleep in Mrs. Flynn's arms and the latter put her into the cot in the kitchen. The time then would be about 20 minutes to 4 o'clock. I served dinner and after Mrs. Flynn and the children had eaten their dinner the latter went out to play. Mrs. Flynn went up and came downstairs a few times and she then handed me the baby (Michael) and told me to feed him and put him in the pram. At about 4:30 p.m. Mrs. Flynn finally went upstairs and did not come down again until about 20 minutes to 6 o'clock. Before going upstairs the last time, Mrs. Flynn gave me directions to feed Philomena when she woke up. She was only a few minutes gone when Philomena awoke and after feeding her I took her out to Maureen, Lizzie and Patricia who were playing on the road. I then washed some tea cloths and the four children Maureen, Lizzie, Patricia and Philomena came in to the kitchen. The time would be then about 5 p.m.. After finishing the washing, I went for the cow. The time would be then about 5:15 p.m.. Before leaving, I prepared the food for the calf and brought it with me to the field where I fed him. When I was leaving the house for the cow, Maureen, Lizzie, Patricia and Philomena were playing between the parlour and the kitchen and the baby (Michael) was asleep in the pram. I found the cow in the field nearest Mrs. Burke's and on the school side of the road. I returned with the cow about 5:30 p.m. and put her in the stable in the back yard. The calf for which I had the food was in the same field as the cow as were other cattle.

When I entered the house after putting the cow in the stable, Maureen, Philomena, Lizzie and Patricia were still playing there and the baby was still asleep. I put down a fire and the baby woke up and I got him a drink. While I was giving him the drink, Mrs. Flynn came downstairs and she took the bottle from me and told me to attend to other work. The other four children were still playing about between the kitchen and the parlour. I am not certain if Philomena was in the house when Mrs. Flynn came downstairs but I think she was. When Mrs. Flynn was downstairs a few minutes I told her there were a few things I wanted from the shop. She said Maureen would do the message but when I told her the articles that were wanted she said that Maureen would not be able to do the message and that I should go myself. She gave me money and when I was leaving for the shop I had the impression that all the children were there. It was then about 5:45 p.m. and I returned from the shop about 6 p.m..

When I entered the yard I saw a child at the window upstairs and I thought it was Philomena. She was saying, 'Ha-ha Mary' to me as I came in from the gate and I spoke up to her. On entering the house and when giving Mrs. Flynn change out of the money she gave me she asked if Philomena was with me and I said, 'No, isn't she upstairs?' I went upstairs immediately and found that Philomena was not there and that the child I thought was Philomena standing at the window when I was returning from the shop was Patricia. I came down and told Mrs. Flynn. I searched the parlour and my own room, but did not find her. Mrs. Flynn and I then searched the yard and outhouses and after not finding her around the house Mrs. Flynn went in the direction of the school and I went towards the chapel in search of Philomena.

I met a couple of Tynan children at the chapel gate and asked them if they seen Philomena and they replied they did not. I also asked the two sisters Sarah and Molly Bergin who were coming out of the chapel if they seen the child. I then entered Miss Carey's where I inquired but could get no tidings of her. Jim Cox who is employed in Carey's said she might be in a field opposite where men were making hay but when I looked into the field I could not see her. I returned to Flynn's. On my way back I met Miss Higgins (Father Walsh's housekeeper) and she had to tidings of the child and as I was approaching Father Walsh's gate I heard Mrs. Flynn crying down the fields opposite the school. I am sure that is where the sound came from. I continued past Flynn's and over the Bridge and I crossed the road fence into Flynn's fields immediately beyond the Bridge.

I saw Mrs. Flynn when I was on top of the fence. She was coming towards the road from the direction of the river. I went to meet her. She asked if had heard anything about the child. I said no. She said, "I searched to the end of the river and could not see her." And then she told me to look for her and find her if I could.

Mrs. Flynn then went towards the road and I crossed the river to search the oat field. I walked around the headland of the oat field and was returning towards the river when I saw a man named John Gorman on the opposite side. He asked if I saw the child and I said I did not. I said that Mrs. Flynn had searched to end of the river but that she did not see the child. Gorman said "we should search there again and make sure." We then continued on down the river, he on his side and I on mine. I was ahead of Gorman and just at the end of the field I saw the child face down in a pool of water. I shouted to Gorman and he took the child out of the water. I was walking on the sandy part of the river bed and was about 5 yards from the child. Gorman brought the child back to the house and I accompanied him. On our way back we met John and Tommy Tynan coming to search for the child and they returned with us.

My reason for bringing the cow in that evening was to milk her. This was the usual practice. And as rule I milked the cow as soon as I brought her in unless the child was crying or there was some urgent work to be done. I did not milk her this evening after bringing her in and she was not milked until near dark. I asked Jes Delaney if he would milk her and Jack Tynan who was also present in the kitchen spoke up and said he would milk her.

I would have milked her earlier only for the excitement of the missing child.

I do not remember meeting any person when I was going for or returning with the cow. About a fortnight previous to this, Philomena followed me when I was going for the cow and she got into the field at the shed. And when I was coming up the field with the cow I heard her crying and brought her home with me. Save on this occasion I never knew the child to wander by herself to this field. There was no fixed hour for bringing home the cow. But as a rule, she was brought in between 4:30 p.m. and 6 p.m. Mr. Flynn returned home that night about 10:00 p.m..

An inquest was held next day and I gave evidence. The day after the inquest my mother came to Mrs. Flynn and told her that I was leaving and that she was sending me to her sister in England. Mr. Flynn said I would have to give a month's notice and my mother agreed to I staying for the month.

A few days after Philomena's death Mrs. Flynn took the three children Maureen, Lizzie and Patricia to Tramore for a fortnight and a week after they left Kate Murray was engaged by Mr. Flynn.

I remember the 22ⁿᵈ day of August. I was still employed at Flynn's. In the house that day were Mr. and Mrs. Flynn, Kate Murray and Maureen, Lizzie, Patricia and the baby, Michael. I was working about the house all day and at about 5:45 p.m. that evening I was preparing the food for the calf. Maureen was with me in the scullery and she brought me the kettle to make the food. She then went into the kitchen where Mrs. Flynn and Kate Murray were seated. While I was preparing the food for the calf, I saw Maureen going through the door leading from the kitchen to the hall. She could have entered the parlour where Mr. Flynn was or gone out the front door but I could not see her after she left the kitchen. This was the last time I saw her alive.

It would be only about five minutes after I saw Maureen going through the kitchen door when I left for the cow and with the food for the calf. When I was going out the gate leading on the road Jack Tynan passed by on a bicycle going in the direction of the school. I found the cow and calf and the other cattle inside the gate just beyond the school and on the same side of the road. I fed the calf and brought home the cow. Save Jack Tynan, I did not see any person on the road when I was going for the cow. When I was returning I met Tom Brophy. He said, 'Good evening Mary' and I returned the salutation. He was the first to speak. He was also cycling in the direction of the Bridge. I met him outside the school gate. When I returned with the cow and put her in the stable I went to the back door. Kate Murray shouted from the kitchen and asked if Maureen was with me. I said, 'No. Wasn't she here when I was leaving?'. Kate replied, 'She is not here now'. I made a search around the back and shouted 'Maureen!' but could not find her and I then milked the cow. After I had milked the cow Kate Murray and the child Lizzie Flynn had returned from Phelan's shop where they had been searching for her but no trace of her could be found. I strained the milk and I then went to Father Walsh's to look for Maureen. I did not get any tidings of her there. Miss Higgins, the housekeeper, was the only person I met there. After coming out on the road from the priest's I went up the road towards Camross village. I spoke to Joe Gleeson who was clipping the hedge. He said, 'I have not seen the child although I am here for two hours but she could have passed unknown to me'. I next entered Carey's and inquired of Miss Carey but found no trace. I next returned to Flynn's. I met Sarah and Molly Bergin coming out from the chapel, but they were unable to give me any tidings of Maureen.

On nearing Flynn's, Mr. Flynn was standing on the road and he asked me if I got any trace of Maureen and I said, 'No'. He then directed me to go back again to Pratt's and inquire. I asked Mrs. Pratt if she saw Maureen but she said she had not. I returned again to Flynn's and Kate Murray directed me to go back to Phelan's dwelling house. On my way to Phelan's I met Greta Higgins and inquired of her but without result. And when I was going in Phelan's lane I asked two boys if they had seen Maureen and they replied they had not. I then went into Phelan's and inquired of Mrs. Phelan and her maid but I could get no tidings there. I remained only a few minutes in Phelan's telling Mrs. Phelan the enquiries I had made. When I came onto the road I met Gould Pratt on a bicycle and he said he had been searching but could get no trace. I returned towards Flynn's and

THE LITTLE RED COAT

as I was passing Matt Gleeson's, Kate Gleeson came out and came down along with me.

We met Joe Gleeson coming up above Father Walsh's gates and Kate asked him if there was any news of Maureen and he said, "It is all over" and he told Kate to go back home, that she was not wanted. Kate said, 'I am a neighbour and I will go down anyway.' I did not realize the child was dead when Joe Gleeson said it was all over.

A few yards further on we met Father Walsh and on Kate Gleeson asking him what was up, he threw his two hands up and replied, 'It's all over'. He added that he had some hope. Kate asked him what had really happened he said that Maureen has been brought in from the river. I got frightened when I heard this and I began to cry and Father Walsh told me to stop crying, that would only upset Mrs. Flynn.

He asked me if Maureen had been upset about Philomena and I said I could not tell. Kate Gleeson and I then went in to Flynn's and Mr. and Mrs. Flynn were in my room with Maureen. There were some other men there as well. I went into the parlour where Kate Murray was and she told me that Mr. Flynn found Maureen in the river.

On the Thursday night after Maureen been buried I was sleeping in my own bedroom on the ground floor at the back of the kitchen. Mr. and Mrs. Flynn went to bed about 10 p.m. and Kate Murray and I went immediately afterwards. I was the only person sleeping downstairs. I fell asleep shortly after going to bed and I did not hear any noise until Mr. Flynn called me at 12:30 a.m.. When I got up I found the parlour on fire and Mr. Flynn told me to get some water. I gave him a bucket of water and he put out the fire. The only place I saw the fire was around the front window. The curtains were completely burned and the wallpaper was also burned. The next morning, I saw that the sofa was burned slightly. There was a fire in the grate in this room during the previous evening but I did not notice if it was alight when the room was on fire.

The following Tuesday night Mr. and Mrs. Flynn retired to bed at about 10 p.m. and Kate Murray and I went to bed shortly afterwards. I slept downstairs and all the others slept upstairs. I fell asleep about ten minutes after getting into bed and I heard nothing unusual until about 1 a.m. when Mr. Flynn called me. He asked me to get water quick and a cloth. I gave him the bucket and a cloth. I thought it was water was in the bucket but I discovered later it was milk. The parlour was on fire in three different places on this occasion. The curtains at the back and front windows were ablaze and the cloth on the sideboard was also burning. *While Mr. and Mrs. Flynn and Kate Murray were endeavouring to put out the fire, the baby began to cry and I was told to go upstairs and mind it. The baby was in Kate Murray's room. Mrs. Flynn came into her room after me and she was crying. She said, "There are ghosts in the house and I will not sleep another night in it."*

She left the room and went downstairs and I heard a noise on the roof of my bedroom which is under the window of Kate Murray's room. There was no one in the latter room at the time only the baby and myself. I thought it was a brick from the top of the house. Mr. and Mrs. Flynn and Kate Murray came up to the room and asked me if I heard anything and I told them I thought something had fallen on to my roof. Mrs. Flynn told me I could sleep in Kate Murray's room that night and I did not go downstairs again. The only child in the house that night was the baby and on the previous occasion of the fire all the children were there but they went to bed upstairs at 7 p.m..

The parlour is on the ground floor and there was a fire in the grate there during the previous evening. I took out the fire and ashes to the kitchen just before Mr. and Mrs. Flynn went to bed. I locked the front and back door before going to bed on the first night the fire occurred but I am not sure whether it was Kate Murray or I locked those doors on the occasion of the second fire.

On the day following the latter fire, my months' notice had expired and I left Flynn's employment.

Signed: Mary Cole
Witness: J. Hunt, Supt.
Witness: D. Twomey, Supt.
Date: 5/11/1927

STATEMENT OF MARY COLE MOUNTRATH BARRACKS

ᔆ

STATEMENT "A" - OCTOBER 3, 1927

I remember 27th July, 1927, the evening on which Philomena Flynn was drowned. Mrs. Flynn went upstairs after dinner—about 3:45 p.m. I did not know that she was going to lie down at this time. I went for the cow at about 5 p.m..

When I was going for the cow, the children were in the parlour. Even though I did not think Mrs. Flynn was asleep, I did not tell her that I was going for the cow. I left the children (4) in the parlour; the baby was asleep in the perambulator in the kitchen. Philomena was in the parlour at the time. The cow, when I found her, was in the field at the school side of the road, and at the far end of the field across the river from the school. I got back to the house at about 5:15 p.m. Philomena was in the kitchen when I got back. Mrs. Flynn had not then come downstairs. She came down about 15 or 20 minutes later. About 10 minutes later, I went to Mr. Phelan's shop for foodstuff for the calf. When I returned, Mrs. Flynn asked me where Philomena was. I said, 'Was that her up on the window?' Mrs. Flynn said, 'Maybe she's upstairs,' and I then went upstairs, but did not find the child, nor was she anywhere in the house. I then went up the road to Tynan's and Carey's to look for the child. Nobody sent me, and Mrs. Flynn would be wrong in stating that she did send me. I was absent about 20 minutes on this errand. When returning at the priest's gate, I heard Mrs. Flynn crying, and I went towards the place where I heard her.

I found her (Mrs. Flynn) in the field on the right hand side of the road, on the far side of the river from the house. She was walking on the bank of the river, and was about the middle of the field, but nearer the road. She said that she had searched down the river, but had failed to find the child. She then told me to look for the child. Mrs. Flynn then returned towards the house, but I am positive that I did not go with her.

She did not tell me to 'look after the children.' I then walked across the river into the oats field, and searched all-round the oats, but did not find the child.

I was walking down the oats towards the river when I saw John Gorman walking down along the opposite bank of the river from the road. At this time, I had not searched any further down than the end of the oats, but Mrs. Flynn had told me that she had searched further down. I walked down the right side of the river, and he (Gorman) went down the left side.

Gorman was ahead of me, and he appeared to be anxious to search down the river. I did not say to him, 'the child must be drowned.' I was not crying. I saw the child in the river, and called out to Gorman. When I shouted, he jumped across the river, and lifted the child. I did not think it strange that though Gorman was ahead of me, and on the opposite bank of the river, he did not see the child first. I thought he was afraid to frighten me. I did not see the child until I got to within four yards of where she lay. It was then I shouted to Gorman.

On Saturday, 30ᵗʰ July, 1927, I remember discussing the drowning with Mrs. Flynn. At no time during this discussion did Mrs. Flynn ask me how it was I happened to be down the river when the child was found, nor did I say to her that I went across to tell Gorman that there was no use in searching down the river.

At no time did I say to Kate Murray that the first I knew of the finding of the child by Gorman was when I saw him stoop down and lift her.

I remember having a conversation with John Gorman on the day of the inquest on Philomena Flynn. I did not ask him what he was going to say concerning the finding of the body. About a fortnight after the inquest I was speaking to him again, but did not refer to the evidence given by him at the inquest. It would be wrong for him to say that I did.

I remember 22ⁿᵈ August, 1927—the evening on which Maureen Flynn was drowned. I was working about the house, and Maureen spent some time with me in my room when I was tidying it up. She was in the room about 5 p.m. and she was talking about what happened when she went out to the bread-man for the bread, and other messages. It would be untrue to say that the bread-man called at 5:30 p.m.. He called between 4:30 p.m. and 5 p.m.. Maureen brought me a kettle of hot water to make the calf's food, and I am positive that she went back into the kitchen again. I made the food in the scullery. Maureen did not follow me out when I went to feed the calf, and bring home the cow. The cow and calf, and the other cattle were in the field beside the school, and near the school gate. When I was coming out at Mr. Flynn's yard gate going for the cow, I saw Jack Tynan, of Camross, passing on a bicycle. I went direct to the field which is about 40 yards away from the gate. When I got to the field, I saw no sign of Maureen. I returned with the cow, having been about 10 minutes away. When I came back Kate

76

Murray asked me where Maureen was. I told her that she wasn't with me, and that I had not seen her. I then milked the cow, and when I had the cow milked, Mr. Flynn told me to go to Fr. Walsh's to see if Maureen was there. I did so, and afterwards, without being told, I went up the road to Carey's, about a quarter mile away. I enquired for Maureen along the way. I remember talking to Joe Gleeson, who was clipping a hedge near the Chapel. He said to me that he had been there for a good while, and had not seen Maureen pass, but that she could have passed unknown to him. He did not say to me that she could not have passed by unknown to him.

When I returned from Carey's, Mrs. Flynn sent me back to make enquiries at Pratt's. Mrs. Pratt had not seen her, and I again returned. I went into the kitchen, and Kate Murray then sent me up to Phelan's to enquire for Maureen. I was away about half-an-hour, and returned. When I returned, Maureen was in the kitchen, apparently dead.

Signed: Mary Cole
Witness: P. Bracken, C/Supt.
Witness: D. Twomey, Supt.
Date: 3/10/1927

CHAPTER TEN

NOVEMBER 16, 1927
MARY COLE IS CHARGED

~

On November 16, 1927, Superintendent Twomey charged Mary Cole with two counts of murder and two counts of arson. In reply to the charges she said, "I do not understand the charges." He then read the charges to her again.

"I don't see how I could be charged with that" was her response.

She was taken before a Peace Commissioner, James Miller, at Mountrath and was remanded to appear before District Justice Meagher at Portlaoise, formerly known as Maryborough, on December 9th.

A newspaper report of the case described the fifteen-year-old as 'looking more like seventeen' who followed the proceedings 'with the keenest interest' and she listened to the narration of Mrs. Flynn 'with perfect composure.'

The State Solicitor was Mr. C. Lavery K.C. and Mary Cole was represented by Mr. W.J. Dwyer, Roscrea.

The charges read by the Clerk (Mr. P. Muldowney) were:

That the defendant did, on the 27th July, 1927, at Camross, in said county, feloniously, and willfully murder Philomena Flynn, aged 1 year and 10 months.

Defendant did on 22nd August, 1927, at Camross, in said county, feloniously, and willfully murder Maureen Flynn, aged 6 years and 10 months.

Defendant did on the night of the 25th, or morning of the 26th August, 1927, at Camross, in said county, unlawfully and feloniously set fire to a dwelling house, the property of Michael Flynn, and did partly destroy same.

Defendant did on the night of the 30th or morning of 31st August, 1927, at Camross, in said county, unlawfully and maliciously set fire to a dwelling house, the property of Michael Flynn, and did partly destroy same.

After describing the events of the two drownings, Statia Flynn spoke about the fires. In her evidence she stated that after the first fire she did not want the fire spoken of as there was talk going about the deaths of the two children. They thought the fire was caused by rats or mice.

On the night of the second fire she went upstairs and spoke to Mary Cole. She told her, "It was not rats or mice that caused this fire; it's spirits," [meaning ghosts]. Mary agreed.

The hearing was adjourned to the following week when Michael Flynn gave his evidence. He told of arriving home from the Rathdowney Show on July 27th to find Philomena dead in his house. He went next day to the river where John Gorman had found her. He told the Court how he found Maureen on the 22nd of August and how afraid she had been of the river two or three days before her death.

He described the events of the fires and added that he never had the lives of his children insured nor had he the house and furniture insured. In reply to Mr. Dwyer he stated that the children and Mary Cole appeared to be fond of each other. Kate Murray, when asked the same question by Mr. Dwyer stated that "Maureen was fond of Mary Cole but Mary Cole was not fond of her."

After evidence by J. Hennessey, Mary Bostick, John Tynan, John Gorman, and Kate Tobin, Mary Cole was returned for trial to the Central Criminal Court.

Application for bail was refused.

Statia's younger sister (Katherine) Kit Fogarty travelled from London to give support to the Flynn family. Aunt Kit had gone into nursing in England and was successful in moving up the ladder at Southampton Hospital. She was a confirmed spinster and developed a reputation for attracting Irish girls who were interested in nursing training at her hospital. She was a strict disciplinarian and kept a firm hold on student nurses under her care. Irish parents were comfortable in placing their daughters under care of Matron Fogarty.

Kit kept newspaper clippings of the hearing in Portlaoise, which became crucial in the early stage of this project.

Upon Mary Cole being remanded for trial in the Central Criminal Court, Kit made plans to return to Dublin for the trial in March the following year.

Aunt Kit Fogarty
— source: *Author's Collection*

Kit, as a hospital Matron, was accustomed to dealing with difficult circumstances and had experience in sorting out personal situations involving her staff in a hospital setting.

When World War II threatened London in 1939, with daily German bombings that often struck hospitals, she volunteered to relieve Matrons in London and was transferred to Whipps Cross Hospital in Leytonstone, outside London where she remained until she retired.

For her service, she was awarded an M.B.E. (Member of the Order of the British Empire) in 1961.

REMAND ORDER RETURNING
MARY COLE FOR TRIAL

(28)" [Wt.P136-Q0.3000.9/24.—A.T & Co.,Ltd.

SAORSTÁT ÉIREANN.

Form 1 a. Certificate of Order.

PETTY SESSIONS (IRELAND) ACT, 1851, 14 & 15 VICT., CAP. 93.

The Attorney-General
at the prosecution of *Complainant.* *Court District of* Maryborough
Supt. D. Twomey, G.S. ,
v
Mary Cole. *Defendant.* *County of* Leix.

*The Words in the Margin in Italics, or Words to the like effect, are to be used according to the circumstances of each case.

(1) CAUSE OF COMPLAINT, with Time and Place. In Ejectments, the Defendant refused to give up to the Plaintiff, Possession of situate at on the Termination of his Tenancy.

I certify, that upon the hearing of a complaint that (¹) *deft.* lid on 27th. July, 1927 at Camross in said County feloniously and wilfully and of malice aforethought, kill and murder Philomena Flynn, aged 1 year and 10 months.

Deft. did on 22nd Aug. 1927 at Camross in said County, feloniously, wilfully and of malice aforethought kill and murder Maureen Flynn, aged 6 years and 10 months.

Deft. did on the night of 25th or morning of 26th. Aug 1927 at Camross in said County unlawfully and maliciously set fire to a dwellinghouse, the property of Michael Flynn and did partly destroy same.

Deft. did on the night of 30th or morning of 31st. Aug. 1927 at Camross in said County unlawfully and maliciously set fire to a dwellinghouse, the property of Michael Flynn and did partly destroy same

an Order was made on the 15ᵗʰ day of December 1927, by

(2) PERSON against whom Order was made. Justice present against (²) Mary Cole
of Derrylahan, Camross, Co. of Leix.

(3) ORDER.
Fine or Debt. To pay to the following Effect, viz. :—(³)
for Fine (or Debt) the Sum of and for Costs the Sum of (forthwith), or (so days) And also in addition or Amd in default of Payment (or distress).
Imprisonment. To be imprisoned for the Period of with (or without) Hard Labour.
Distrainal. To be levied from said premises in days, and pay the sum of to the Complainant for Costs.
Dismissal. That this Complaint be dismissed on the Merits (or without Prejudice) and that he do pay the sum of to the Defendant for Costs.

Deft. returned for trial, in custody, to the next Sitting of the Central Criminal Court to be held in Dublin.

Signed, William Clayle

District Justice of said County.

This 15ᵗʰ day of December, 1927.

— *Source: Trial File Document 1927*

CHAPTER ELEVEN

MARCH 20, 1928
THE TRIAL BEGINS

&

AUTHOR'S NOTE:

The following account of the trial of Mary Cole is consistent with reports from the *Irish Independent,* March 21, 22, 23, 24, 1928, and *The Irish Times,* March 23, 24, 1928. These newspaper clippings were found among Aunt Kit's belongings upon her death in 1996.

&

The trial opened before Mr. Justice John O'Byrne and a jury of twelve men at the Central Criminal Court, Green Street, Dublin, at 11 a.m. on Tuesday, March 20, 1928. The jury had been sworn on Tuesday, February 7, 1928.

The State prosecutors were Mr. William Carrigan, K.C. and Mr. Dudley White, K.C. The Defence was Mr. James J. Walsh (instructed by Mr. William Dwyer, solicitor, Roscrea).

Mary Cole pleaded "not guilty" to two charges of murder and two counts of arson.

Mr. Carrigan drew His Lordship's attention to the form of the Indictment which embraced offences for felony and misdemeanour which was so framed under the Indictments Act 1925—and the Criminal Justice Amendment Act 1924 provisions, and asked the Court to consider whether both classes of offence should be tried together or separately. Mr. Walsh stated he raised no formal objection to the trial proceeding on the entire indictment.

Mr. Justice O'Byrne ruled that Mary Cole be tried on the two murder charges only.

The County Registrar then gave the prisoner in charge on the said 1st and 2nd Counts of murder, the Jury having been sworn to try the issue on these Counts only.

Mr. Carrigan, K.C. opened the case for the prosecution at 12:40 p.m.. He stated, "This was the most extraordinary case that could be submitted to a jury. The children's parents had no suspicion that they were murdered by the accused until certain incidents occurred and the girl left their employment."

"The girl in the dock is a girl of an unnatural kind—a girl with a powerful but disordered intellect. One of the baffling proofs of her skill and unnatural ingenuity was that neither the local police and doctors who attended the inquests on the children, or the parents, for a moment suspected that the children had come to their end by anything else than the merest accident."

He described the 'ugly incident' of the night spent in the car and the confrontation that followed.

"Of such a nature was she that she was able to disarm all suspicion on the part of Mr. Flynn and his wife who felt that they had done a good and kindly act, and that the girl had learned her lesson, and had fallen into her place again much relieved and comforted."

"On the contrary, from that time forth the girl watched her opportunity to take a terrible revenge upon her employers."

Mr. Carrigan showed the jury a photograph of the location where Philomena was found, stating, "It must have done what would require a person of strength and agility to do, penetrate a thicket of wood, pass a barbed wire fencing and there at the river meet its death. The only other way the child could have reached the spot was by another path or route past a gate and got into the field where the cow was, and thence to the river bank. But the jury would estimate the seeming impossibility for all this to have been done by an infant of one year and ten months. In the latter case the gate would require to have been lifted and pushed."

"The jury would undoubtedly, when all the facts were laid before them, hold that the little one could not have accomplished such a feat of strength, and it would be shown that the body was found in an extremely shallow piece of water."

In the case of the drowning of Maureen, who was last seen with Mary Cole in the scullery, Mr. Carrigan contended, "The girl would have had to go through a gate and over a field with the knowledge of the prisoner." He also said, "The poor child's head must have been held under the water which was only eight inches deep at that point."

He told the jury that they would hear that "Mary Cole was seen in the field with a child who was wearing a red coat, a field into which the infant could never have got by itself. But Mary Cole denied that she ever took out the child that evening. Why did she deny it?".

"When the body was found the red coat was not on it, and the theory was that Mary Cole took the red coat and brought it back to the house to sustain her case of denial that she was with the child at all."

"The bruises on the foreheads of the children were apparently caused by pressing the heads down whilst the bodies of the victims were over the water."

"The jury would have before them evidence, that the accused, young in years, but with the mind of an adult, who was capable of using strong language ascribing the misfortunes of the Flynn family to their having had her character taken away from her by their charges made against her. It was clear that it was a case of revenge being taken by the accused."

"The jury should know that, unlike past cases of the kind, capital punishment did not at present apply to persons under 16 years of age."

Statia Flynn was called and described the events of the end of June and the evening when Mary Cole confessed to her indiscretion after a number of strong denials. The pleadings of Fr. Walsh resulted in Mary's continued employment at the Flynn's. Then on July 27th Philomena disappeared and was later found drowned.

The first day's hearing also dealt with introducing maps and photographs of the scenes of the drownings. A wooden model of the Master's House was introduced by Sergeant Leo McGrath, of the Garda Headquarters. Garda Myles Saul entered as evidence the *Book of Photographs*.

CHAPTER TWELVE

MARCH 21, 1928
STATIA FLYNN IS
CROSS-EXAMINED

❧

The second day, Statia Flynn continued her evidence, describing what happened on August 22, 1927.

The red coat was produced by Mr. White. Statia identified it as belonging to Philomena and stated that none of the other children had a red coat.

She said that when she came down from her room on July 27th she understood the cow had not been milked and learned later that it had been. After the drowning, when she again asked Mary Cole when she last saw Philomena she told her, "She was there when I milked the cow," pointing to the front door.

On cross-examination by Mr. Walsh, she was asked, "Was it usual for you to tell this girl in detail everything she had to do?"

"Now and again I would have to remind her of it."

"Would there be anything unusual in her going out on her own to bring in the cow to be milked?"

"There would."

"The cow could not be brought in without your authority?".

"If I or my husband were not there she was not to go out for the cow."

"When was that understanding come to?"

"From the first day she was told that she was never to leave the children by themselves."

"Didn't the children often go up to Tynan's to play with other children?"

"If they got permission to go."

"Did the children, to your knowledge, ever wander some distance away from the house?"

"Never."

"Did the accused ever say to you that Philomena was found

87

by her some distance from the house near the bank of the river?"

"Yes, but she did not say near the bank of the river."

Mr. Justice O'Byrne: "When was that?"

"On the 15th of July."

Mr. Walsh: "About ten days before the first drowning?"

"Yes."

"Mary Cole came to you and said that she found Philomena a considerable distance away from the house?"

"She gave me that version then, but a different one later."

Mr. Justice O'Byrne: "What did she say to you on July 15th?"

"She was out on a message, and when she came in she said that as she was coming down the road she looked over the ditch, and saw Philomena going straight down the field."

Mr. Walsh: "Did she say anything else?"

"She said that she must have got into the field at the shed where a tree had been cut." She then said that the prisoner told her she followed Philomena down the field and brought her back. She believed at that time that the child had got into the field but she didn't believe it now. Later she asked the prisoner in what direction the child was going and she replied, "down the river."

"What did you say?" asked counsel.

"I said 'Oh my God! Why didn't you tell me that at first and I could have gone down there?' I then asked the prisoner what part of the river, and she replied 'To the part where she was found.' The prisoner never mentioned the river before that day."

"She told you that the child was going in the direction of the river?"

"Yes, and also that she would not have known that the child was there only her attention was drawn to it."

"At all events, on July 15th the prisoner said she found the child in the field?"

"Yes."

"And this field is a considerable distance from your house?"

"Yes."

"Did you ever know of Philomena being away some distance from the house?"

"Never alone."

"Isn't it possible that if she went off playing with other children she could have wandered off?"

"It is."

"You came downstairs at six o'clock?"

"Yes, when the Angelus was ringing."

"And the prisoner was then giving the baby his milk?"

"Yes."

"You say you told her to go for the cow and she replied that she wanted some foodstuff for the calf?"

"Yes."

"You gave her some money for this, and she went and got it?"

"Yes."

"She was out of the house about five minutes?"

"Yes."

"I think it is clear now that the cow was milked in the house?"

"Yes, at that time."

"You recollect the incident in connection with which the Parish Priest was brought to your house?"

"Yes."

"Her manner was unusual for a fortnight and even after that she was not quite satisfactory? From June well into July she was not, according to you, doing her duty properly?"

"No."

"But after that she was quite happy and bright?"

"She wasn't as sullen as before."

"Didn't her sullenness simply amount to a certain amount of childish shame about this incident of the boys?"

"No."

"For a fortnight you were not as friendly with her?"

"No."

"But long before Philomena's death you were quite friendly and bright with her?"

"I was not as fond of her as before."

"Mr. Carrigan tells us the wise priest administered a different sort of caution to these young blackguards in the locality who had been with this girl?"

"Yes, I heard that."

"It was a very different sort of caution to the one that he administered to Mary Cole?"

"I don't know what caution he administered to them."

Mr. Carrigan: "If Mr. Walsh wants to bring out names and details in connection with these incidents they can be brought out."

Mr. Walsh: "You have seen the spot where Maureen was drowned?"

"I do not know the exact spot."

"It is some distance to the rere [rear] of your house?"

"I know the direction."

"You told us that Maureen came into the kitchen, took a kettle from the fireplace, and then went to the door, called after somebody and went out?"

"Yes, and I never saw her alive again."

"Up till that time, Mary Cole was in the scullery?"

"Yes."

"And twenty-two minutes later you again saw Mary Cole?"

"About that; when she was coming from Pratt's, where she had been looking for Maureen."

"Did you tell her to go to Pratt's?"

"No. I think it was my husband."

"How far is Pratt's from your place?"

"About five minutes' walk. She was milking the cow when my husband sent her to Pratt's."

"Where was the cow?"

"In the house."

"How long had she been milking the cow when your husband told her to go to Pratt's?"

"About two minutes."

"This milking of the cow and going to Pratt's all took place within twenty-five minutes?"

"Yes, Mary Cole was out about twenty minutes before she came back with the cow."

"You say that from the time she returned with the cow, was told by your husband to go to Pratt's, went there and came back took the remainder of the 25 minutes?"

"Yes."

"Mary Cole left your employment on August 31st?"

"Yes. Her mother said she was thinking of sending Mary to England and I said I hoped it was not on account of what happened."

"You gave her a little present when she was leaving?"

"Yes."

ADAPTED ORDNANCE MAP OF CAMROSS
WITH LEGEND SHOWING KEY LOCATIONS

KEY

1. Master's House
2. National School
3. Parochial House
4. Phelan's
5. Pratt's
6. Tynan's
7. Carey's Post Office
8. Bridge
9. Longford Cross

"A" Site of Philomena
"G" Site of Maureen

House to "G" = 245

Location numbering by Author
Ordinance Map — *source: Trial Evidence 1928*

CHAPTER THIRTEEN

MARCH 21, 1928
CROSS-EXAMINATION OF
MICHAEL FLYNN

❧

On Wednesday, March 21, 1928, Michael Flynn corroborated the evidence given by his wife in connection with the visit of the Parish Priest to his house in June 1927.

He told Mr. Lavery, that on July 27, 1927, there was a crop of high-growing oats in the field where Philomena was found. At one place the field could be entered over the stump of an old tree that had been cut down a few months before. On the road side the distance of the top of the stump from the level of the road was two and a half feet, and there was on the other side a slope of five feet to the field. He also gave particulars of the nature of the bank of the stream where Philomena was drowned.

A person going to the stream by the oat field would have to get through the fence of two strands of barbed wire.

There was a fairly thick growth of furze bushes on the bank of the river. He would say it would be impossible for a very young child to get through the furze.

EVENTS OF AUGUST 22, 1927

Michael was in the house all day because it was raining. At about 5:25 p.m. he was reading in the parlour, and on looking through the window he saw Mary Cole with a bucket in her hand cross the front yard in the direction of the field on the other side of the road. He took it that she was going to feed the calf. He remained in the parlour until he saw her bringing the cow from the field.

Mr. Justice O'Byrne: "How long was that from the time you saw her looking up the road?"

"It would be a quarter of an hour to twenty minutes."

Continuing, he stated that he remained in the parlour until he heard Kate Murray, the other servant, say that Maureen was missing. He then described the search for her in which Mary Cole joined.

He himself found the child lying in the stream with her face in the water where it was eight or nine inches deep. Her face was red, there was froth in her mouth, and she appeared to be dead.

When he had carried her home, he saw a black bruise on her forehead. The bed of the stream where the body lay was stony. Shortly after the discovery, he asked Mary Cole where she had found the cow, and she said it was the extreme end of the farm.

In cross-examination by Mr. Walsh, Mr. Flynn said that at one side of the river the land was flat and when he spoke to Mary Cole as to where the cattle had been she said at the farthest part of the land on the school-house side. He, however, saw no cattle there at the time. There were large and small stones at the points of the river near where the body was found, and, the stream being shallow there, it would be easier to cross.

"Does not the road rise somewhat steep at the side?"

"At one point, yes."

"You saw Mary Cole walking towards the main road and turning to look around?"

"Yes."

"Anybody might do that?"

"Yes."

"When you spoke to her next do you know whether she had been milking the cow?"

"She was only a short time away, and I told her to go and look for Maureen. Fifteen minutes had elapsed."

"Was she actually milking the cow when you told her to look for Maureen?"

"She was at the place where the cow was."

"You knew Mary Cole in your school?"

"Yes."

"And she knew your children?"

"Yes."

"When your servant she was fond of the children?"

"Yes."

"And the children fond of her?"

"Yes."

Mr. Flynn, in reply to His Lordship, stated that he could not remember the exact words used when the accused told him on August 22nd that she had found the cow at the extreme end of the farm.

Mr. Flynn, recalled by Mr. Justice O'Byrne, said there was nothing unusual in the condition of Philomena's clothes on July 15th, when according to Mary Cole, she was wandering by herself in the field leading to the river.

CHAPTER FOURTEEN

MARCH 21, 1928
EYEWITNESSES TESTIFY

આ

After Michael Flynn's evidence, John Gorman was called. He related being told by Mrs. Flynn that Philomena was missing and when he went searching he met Mary Cole to the right of the river.

"Did she say anything to you?"

"She said that Phil was missing for an hour and a half."

"Did she say anything else?"

"She said something like wouldn't it be an awful thing if she was drowned?"

"What did you say then?"

"I asked her was the child ever at the river before? And she said something I could not catch."

He went on to say that he proceeded to go along one bank of the river, with Mary Cole walking in front of him on the other bank. When they had gone about hundred yards she called out that the child was in the water. At that time, she was twenty yards in front of him. Witness jumped across the river to the other side.

Mr. Carrigan: "Had Mary Cole gone to the edge of the water when you got up?"

"She went to within two or three yards of where the child was lying and then she ran away for about fifteen yards, where she stood."

"How deep was the water where the child lay?"

"About sixteen inches."

"How much of the body was covered in the water?"

"All of it. There was about three inches of water over the whole of the body."

"Did you say anything to Mary Cole?"

"I called her back to assist me in trying to restore the child's life."

"Did she come?"

"No. She stood where she was."

"What did you do next?"

"I saw that the child was dead, and I carried her to the house."

"Where did Mary Cole go?"

"She came with me."

Mr. Walsh: "When Mary Cole spoke to you did she seem like a person genuinely looking for the child?"

"Yes."

"When she shouted 'There's the child,' did she see terrified?"

"She seemed excited."

"And for a moment stood still?"

"Yes."

"Was she excited and apparently upset?"

"Yes."

Dr. Phelan said he saw at Mr. Flynn's house the dead body of a two-year-old female child (Philomena). There was discolouration on the skin of the right forehead. Death was due to asphyxia caused by drowning.

Dr. McCarthy said he saw the body of Maureen Flynn. He found a bruise that was made during the child's lifetime. This bruise had been caused by external violence of some sort; he should say by contact with a blunt object. The mouth and eyes were partly open, and the skin was of a bluish tint. Death was due to drowning.

Mr. Walsh asked Dr. McCarthy: "How long would it be necessary to keep the child's head under nine inches of water in order to do away with her?"

"I think about half a minute's immersion would be sufficient to cause death. It is very hard to be certain. It depends upon the victim."

John Hennessey stated that on the evening of July 27, 1927 he was driving to Camross when he saw "the Master's maid" in a field by the roadside driving a cow.

Mr. Carrigan: "Was there anybody with her?"

"There was a little child with her."

"How was that child dressed?"

"In a red coat."

"How far away were the girl and the child from you?"

"They were about six or seven perches [33-38 yards] in the field."

He identified the prisoner as the girl he saw with the child.

Shortly after that she came into Phelan's shop for calf meal while he was there.

Cross-examined by Mr. Walsh the witness said he saw a girl and a little child in a field. The child was wearing a red coat, and was running alongside the girl who was driving Mr. Flynn's cow. He went on to Phelan's shop and a short time afterwards the same girl, (the prisoner) came into the shop and bought linseed meal.

"The girl and the child were coming towards the gate of a field leading to the public road when you passed by that evening?"

"Yes."

Mary Bostic, examined by Mr. Lavery, said on the evening of July 27th as she was proceeding home with her brother she saw the prisoner driving a cow about nine or ten yards from the gate of a field near Longford Cross. That was then nearing 6:00 p.m.. She had been to Phelan's shop. On her way to the shop she didn't see anybody in the field.

Cross-examined by Mr. Walsh, the witness stated that the previous witness was traveling the road about a quarter of a mile in front of her.

John Tynan, thirteen-years-old, stated he saw Maureen Flynn in front of the school on the evening that she was drowned. Maureen was coming from the direction of her parents' house, and he saw the prisoner leave the house at the same time.

On that evening, he milked Flynn's cow. Mary Cole asked another man to milk the cow for her. Witness was present at the time and this man turned the job over to him.

Cross-examined by Mr. Walsh, the boy said this was the first time he had mentioned about the milking of the cow.

Kate Tobin gave evidence of conversations she had with Mary Cole subsequent to the drowning of the children. One of the statements made by her was that when there was an outbreak of fire at Mr. Flynn's house, she saw a brush going out through the window, and she also said that ghosts had taken the milk.

Mr. Corrigan: "Did she tell you anything about how

Philomena came to be drowned?"

"She told me that when she was going for the cow, she left Philomena playing with the other children in the parlour."

"Did she describe the disappearance of Maureen?"

"She told me that Maureen wanted to accompany her when she went for the cow but she would not take her because the little girl was too fond of telling tales. When she came back with the cow Maureen was missing."

"Did she tell you anything about Mrs. Flynn?"

"She said Mrs. Flynn was a hard woman to take away from her the costume she had given her."

"Did she say anything else that Mrs. Flynn had done to her?"

"She told me that if Mrs. Flynn had brought the priest on her twice she had two inquests in the house afterwards."

"Did she say anything about insurance?"

"She told me that the children were insured, and Mr. Flynn had got £50 for Philomena but would get nothing for Maureen because it was too soon after the other case."

"Did she say anything about any purchase by the Flynn's?"

"I said I heard that Mr. Flynn had bought Burke's farm and she said, 'and well they could buy it.'

In cross-examination, the witness stated that she is now in the service of Mr. and Mrs. Flynn in their new home in Tipperary and she had discussed the case with them frequently.

After the adjournment on March 21st, the Jury asked that they might be afforded some little entertainment for the evening. The Judge ordered "the Sheriff to arrange for a Bus Drive for the Jury."

CHAPTER FIFTEEN

MARCH 22, 1928
EVIDENCE CONTINUES

෮

Chief Superintendent Peter Bracken stated that the accused made a statement at the barracks accounting for her movements and in reply to questions put to her. She signed that statement which was dated October 3, 1927.

Superintendent Hunt said the prisoner visited Mountrath Barracks on the evening of November 4, 1927 in response to his message. He told her that he wished to take a statement in writing from her in connection with the deaths of the Flynn children. She was not then under arrest, had not been charged, and no inducement or threat was held out to her. The statement was made in reply to questions the witness put to the girl. When he had written the statement he read it over to the prisoner, sentence by sentence, and she said it was right.

Superintendent Bracken said he interrogated the accused at the barracks in Mountrath. She had come there with him voluntarily and she made a statement. She was arrested on November 15, 1927.

That statement, a very lengthy one, which was read by Mr. Dudley White, K.C. conveyed the girl's story of what happened on July 27th and August 22nd.

In reply to Mr. Walsh, the witness stated that the statement was written down from a series of answers given by her to a series of questions put by him to her.

Thomas Brophy, the Parish Priest's servant, in reply to Mr. Carrigan, stated that about ten days before Philomena was drowned, he found her in a field alongside the road. She was standing at the bottom of the fence on the field side, some five feet from the top of the fence, and she was crying. That was the only occasion that he saw the child wandering.

The place he found her was close to the stump of an ash tree that had been growing on the top of the fence. While he was pacifying the child Mary Cole came up the field driving the cow.

Mr. Walsh, (for the prisoner): "Did Mrs. Flynn in her deposition in the Court at Maryborough say one word that she knew that the child had been found astray in the field?"

"I am sure that she did."

"And in your deposition you did not say one single word about this important incident. I suggest that the reason why it is introduced here today because for the first time I brought it out in the cross-examination of Mrs. Flynn yesterday."

Witness: "I gave it in my statement to the Superintendent."

In reply to Mr. Walsh, he stated the fence near the spot was lower there than anywhere else along the road boundary of the field.

Joe Delaney, examined by Mr. Dudley White said the prisoner came into Phelan's shop in which he was an assistant at 5:40 p.m. (old time) on July 27th and bought calf meal. She was there about two minutes. A short time prior to that he saw three of the Flynn children pass the shop from the direction of their own house.

Kate Murray, a housekeeper employed by Mrs. Flynn, said the prisoner complained to her several times of her mistress in bringing the Parish Priest to her in connection with her relations with boys. She seemed to resent this very much and spoke of her character having been taken away owing to this calling in of the Parish Priest.

On the evening of August 22nd, the witness was working in the kitchen. The prisoner was preparing food for the calf in the scullery. Maureen was with her there. After a short time, Maureen came into the kitchen, left a kettle on the fire, and went out. The witness never saw the child alive again.

The prisoner left the house by the backyard carrying a bucket, and a few minutes later witness missed Maureen. She looked for her around the house and outbuildings, but could not find her. She then took it for granted that the child had gone with the prisoner to bring in the cow. The prisoner returned with the cow sometime later.

The Judge: "About how long was that from the time Mary Cole had gone out?"

"About 15 or 20 minutes."

Mr. Carrigan: "Did you say anything to Mary Cole when she came in?"

"I only asked her if the child was with her, and then I went to Phelan's shop to see if she was there. When I came back, Mary Cole was in the cowshed."

Cross-examined by Mr. Walsh she stated that she went into the employment of the Flynns on August 6th and she was still with them in Tipperary. She never discussed the case with them.

"Do you mean to tell the jury that since August last year you never mentioned this case to the Flynns?"

"We never went through the case."

"Kate Tobin told us yesterday that they went through the case with her, and you today say that they did not discuss it with you?"

"I knew nothing about it."

"You say that Mary Cole came back in about 15 or 20 minutes after she went out with the bucket to feed the calf?"

"Yes."

"When did Mary Cole start making complaints about Mrs. Flynn?"

"Now and again she would begin talking about Mrs. Flynn calling in the priest on her."

"When Maureen's dead body was brought in and placed on Mary Cole's bed, did it occur to you that there was anything strange about the place?"

"No."

"Did you go to Mrs. Flynn and tell her that while she was away in Tramore Mary Cole was making complaints about her?"

"I did not."

"And it was only when the mystery was revived in October or November that you thought of these complaints of Mary Cole?"

"It was not. It was always on my mind."

"When did you let it out of your mind?"

"I can't say."

Re-examined by Mr. Carrigan, the witness stated that Mary Cole told her that Jack Tynan told her that on the evening she was drowned he saw Maureen going into the field after her when she was going for the cow. Witness asked her how it was she had not seen the child and she only a short distance in front of her and she replied that she did not see her.

To Mr. Walsh she stated that the conversations with Mary Cole took place on the day of the inquest on Maureen or the day after it.

"So we can say that your suspicions were aroused on the day of the inquest?"

"No sir."

Judge: "That is a matter for the jury."

Superintendent Patrick Sheridan gave evidence that the distance from Flynn's gate to the spot where Maureen was drowned was two hundred and forty-five yards, and by the oat field to where the body of Philomena was found was three hundred and nineteen yards.

Superintendent Twomey, Abbeyleix, gave evidence of arrest. He said he charged her with the willful murder of Philomena Flynn and Maureen Flynn, and cautioned her. She replied: "I don't understand the charges."

He read the charges over a second time and then she said: "I don't see how I can be charged with that."

This closed the case for the prosecution.

Mr. Walsh formally applied for a direction, which was dismissed.

"I will now call Mary Cole."

CHAPTER SIXTEEN

MARCH 22, 1928
MARY COLE IS EXAMINED
BY COUNSEL

❧

HER OWN STORY

Looking cool and self-possessed, the girl left the dock and took her seat in the witness chair, facing the jury. Glancing at some friends in Court, she smiled, and then devoted her whole attention to the questions of her counsel.

Her appearance and behaviour on the witness table were one of the most remarkable features of this extraordinary case.

Speaking in a pleasant tone of voice, she was quite at ease under the severe cross-examination of Mr. Carrigan, never got excited, and never lost the thread.

For the most part she answered simply "yes" or "no" and did so after carefully listening to the question.

When a fuller explanation was necessary she gave it clearly and briefly. She was quite at home when explaining the *locus in quo*, the place in question, on the large ordnance map.

She said she was fifteen last November and was born in Camross, where her parents resided. She was the eldest of seven children. She went to Flynn's school when she was seven, and attended until she was about fourteen. She knew Maureen Flynn and Eilis Flynn before she left school.

Mr. Walsh: "Do you recollect being engaged as domestic servant by Mrs. Flynn?"

"Yes, that was in September 1926, a few months after I left school."

"Am I right in saying that from the time you arrived at Flynn's you were quickly given to understand that you were to be a maid of all work?"

"Yes."

"You were doing all the work of the place?"

"I was."

"Mr. Flynn, I think, kept a cow?"

"Yes, he had three."

"Milking cows?"

"Yes."

"Was it your duty to milk three cows or only one?"

"Mostly I had to do the three."

"You always had to milk one?"

"Yes."

"Mr. Flynn's land lies, I think, on either side of the road and is intersected by a river?"

"Yes."

"Is the land just to the left rere of the house on the right bank of the river plot or what?"

"It gradually slopes to the bank of the river."

"Is there a decline in the road from the front gate to the bridge, do you go down a hill towards the bridge?"

"There's a slope."

"Does the land on the left of that road correspondingly slope?"

"Yes."

"What is the land on the school side like?"

"A big hill up over the river."

"Does it rise suddenly from the bed of the river?"

"It goes up very suddenly."

"Were the cows free to wander from the land on the left of the road to the land on the right?"

"Yes, you would get them everywhere."

"What were your duties in Flynn's house?"

"I had to do all the housework, and had care of the baby."

"Had you to look after the other children?"

"Occasionally."

"What was your usual time for getting up in the morning?"

"I had to be in the kitchen at seven, light the fire, and cook the breakfast. I had to milk the cow before that and feed the calf. I also had to dress the children, give them their porridge and make their breakfast. At eight o'clock I got the workman's breakfast ready."

"Now, when the children went to school, what had you to do?"

"I had to clean up, and take care of the baby."

"Anything else?"

"Yes, I also had to do the bedrooms, clean the parlour and do all the housework, and of course, I was responsible for the baby when Mrs. Flynn was at school."

"That baby was left in your care?"

"All through the year 1926."

"I think Mr. and Mrs. Flynn were quite kind to you?"

"Yes, they were very good."

"You never had any difference with Mr. or Mrs. Flynn until March of 1927?"

"No."

Mary Cole said that Mrs. Flynn threatened to tell her mother that she saw her talking to boys when she went out in the evenings. In the following June, Mrs. Flynn again accused her of being with boys and of being out all night with a boy. The witness denied it then. She did, in fact, leave her bedroom one morning and stay out from four to six o'clock with a boy. She subsequently admitted this to Mrs. Flynn before the Parish Priest was brought to the house.

"Am I right in saying that you made this admission to Mrs. Flynn in the kitchen before the Parish Priest actually came on the scene?"

"He had been there the previous evening."

"Did he interview you on that occasion?"

"He interviewed three boys."

"Did he interview you on the first occasion?"

"No."

"Following the interview with the three boys did another parade of boys take place before the Parish Priest at the house?"

"Yes, it was arranged."

"While the priest was interviewing the boys where were you?"

"In the kitchen with Mrs. Flynn."

"Did you then admit to Mrs. Flynn that you had left your

bedroom and stayed with a boy?"

"Yes."

"And in your presence she told the priest that you had been with this boy? I think after some further discussion the Parish Priest asked her to take pity on you and to keep you?"

"Yes, he asked her to be a mother to me."

"She agreed to keep you?"

"Yes."

"Now, before I leave this matter, were there any improper relations between you and the boy on that morning between 4:00 and 6:00 a.m.?"

"No sir; we had no improper relations with each other that morning."

"Did you hear Mrs. Flynn's evidence?"

"I did."

"She took a costume from you that she had given you?"

"Yes."

"Did you mind very much when she took this costume from you?"

"No sir."

"You were feeling rather ashamed about this whole business with the boys?"

"I was."

" Did you in point of fact go down on your knees and ask Mrs. Flynn to forgive you?"

"Yes."

"After the priest had been brought Mrs. Flynn tells us she was a bit cool with you for a fortnight?"

"She was not really cool, but not as friendly."

"She tells us that you were silent and sullen?"

"I was not. I tried to please her in every way."

"At the end of a fortnight the coolness passed away, she says, and you were much brighter?"

"We were just the same as ever then."

"That would be about the middle of July?"

"Yes."

Continuing her direct evidence after lunch, Mary Cole stated that Mrs. Flynn returned from school at 3:30 p.m. on July 27th, and had dinner, which had been prepared by the witness. After dinner she went upstairs to rest, leaving instructions that Philomena was to get her dinner when she woke up. She did so, and Philomena then joined the other children who were out on the road playing. The witness tidied up after the dinner, and resumed the weekly chores. Part of her duties was to do the week's washing.

Mr. Walsh: "Do you identify this red coat?"

"Yes, it was the children's coat."

"Did you do anything with that coat on Wednesday, July 27th?"

"I washed it."

To Mr. Justice O'Byrne she stated, "At lunch that day Mrs. Flynn gave me the coat to wash as she wanted it for the child, Pat, when they were going on their holidays in a few days. She had the coat washed when Mrs. Flynn came home at 3:30 p.m.."

Mr. Carrigan: "Mrs. Flynn was not asked about that."

Continuing, she stated that she finished the housework and went out to bring in the cow. All the children, including Philomena, were in the house when she went out. Shortly after she got back to the house, Mrs. Flynn came downstairs and sent her to Phelan's for messages. She did not know that Mrs. Flynn was lying down that afternoon. Returning from Phelan's she saw one of the Flynn's waving at her from a top window of their house. When she got back to the kitchen, Mrs. Flynn asked her had she seen Philomena, and she replied that she was upstairs. She went up and found that it was the other little girl, Pat.

She then described the search carried out for the missing child until she met John Gorman on one bank of the river while she was on the other side. Both went down the river, until she saw the white clothes of a child in the river partly covered by the water.

Mary shouted to Gorman, and then being terrified, ran a little distance further down, and stood there.

She came back when Gorman called to her, but not quite up to where he was trying to revive the child.

Further questioned by Mr. Walsh, she stated that she usually went out for the cow without being told by Mr. or Mrs. Flynn to do so. She did not remember meeting or seeing anyone on the road while she was out for the cow that evening.

"Do you recollect having your attention drawn to the fact on one occasion that one of the children was alone in the field?"

"Yes."

"And that the priest's man who was on the road called your attention to it?"

"Yes."

"And you brought the child home?"

"Yes."

"You gave evidence at the inquest?"

"Yes."

"And you were present when a conversation took place between Mrs. Flynn and your mother?"

"Yes."

"And some time after that Mrs. Flynn went to Tramore?"

"Yes, with some of the children."

"Who were left in the house?"

"Myself and the baby and Mr. Flynn and afterwards Kate Murray."

"After that you had a conversation about the death of Philomena?"

"Yes."

"With Kate Murray?"

"Yes."

"What did she say?"

"She said she did not hear all, and she wanted to hear all."

"Is it a fact that you made a complaint about Mrs. Flynn?"

"No."

"Did you complain to Kate Murray at all about Mrs. Flynn's attitude to you?" Did you harbour any ill will against Mrs. Flynn for her attitude to you?"

"No."

"It is stated that when you were seen going out on the road and beyond the school wall you turned around and looked in the direction of the school. Is that so?"

"No. I passed on and by the gate at the school wall, and to

where the cattle were and I fed the calf."

"When Maureen was missed you made every inquiry you possibly could?"

"Yes."

"You spoke to everyone you met?"

"Yes."

"You remained on in their employment?"

"Yes."

"Had you any hand, act, or part in the drowning of these children?"

"None."

"You were fond of them?"

"Yes."

"And they were fond of you?"

"Yes." (The witness displayed emotion in replying to these questions.)

"You heard the evidence as to your having been seen with one of the children crossing the field, and that the child wore a red cloak?"

"No, it is a mistake."

"You know Kate Tobin?"

"Yes, she was at school with me."

"Had you any conversation with her about the death of these children?"

"Yes."

"In her evidence did you hear her speak about insurance money?"

"Yes"

"Was that true?"

"No, but she said that the insurance people were looking up about the death of the little children."

The examination of the accused had lasted for two and a half hours.

The prisoner, who looks older than she says she is, stated that she was not in the field with a child wearing a red coat.

Mr. Carrigan: "When John Hennessey thought that he saw you in the field with a child wearing a red coat, his eyes were deceiving him?"

Mary Cole: "It is possible."

"Miss Murray says you found the cow in the ferns at the end of the field?"

"I don't recollect ever telling her that. She must be making a mistake."

"And Mr. Flynn is making a mistake?"

"He is not telling the truth."

Replying to cross-examination by Mr. Carrigan, Mary Cole said she did not believe in spirits or ghosts, but Kate Tobin did. It was on the night of August 15th that the brush "flew out of the window" as she had described it in connection with the girl Tobin. There was commotion in Flynn's house that night. A loud crash was heard during the night when a fire was being extinguished.

"Did you represent to the family, who were all confused, that there were ghosts in the house?"

"No."

"Was Mrs. Flynn terrified when you said that the brush flew through the window?"

"No. I meant that the wind could have blown it off the window sill."

Replying to further cross-examination by Mr. Carrigan, she said Kate Tobin told her Mr. Flynn had got £50 of insurance money over the first child. She denied having ever said to Kate Tobin that the reason the Flynns did not get two sums of insurance money was because the second child's death took place too soon after that of the first.

She and Mrs. Flynn got along very well together until the trouble over the boys when the Parish Priest was brought in. Until the priest was brought in she denied to Mrs. Flynn that there was any foundation for the charges in connection with her conduct with boys. She now realised that it was improper for her to leave her room and be alone with a boy in the early hours of the morning, but she saw nothing wrong with it at the time.

On the Saturday following her confession about her conduct, Mrs. Flynn and her mother had a serious conversation about Mary. Her mother reprimanded her daughter very severely for her conduct.

"Did Mrs. Flynn say to your mother that if she (your mother) got you employment without telling your new employer what had happened, she (Mrs. Flynn) would deem it her duty to tell your employer what sort of girl you were?"

"Yes."

To Mr. Justice O'Byrne: "I did not see my father when I went home on the Sunday after the priest had come to the house."

Mr. Carrigan: "You say that after that incident you had no grievance against Mrs. Flynn?"

"I had not, sir."

"And it is not true for Kate Murray to say that you complained about Mrs. Flynn exposing you to the priest and taking away your character?"

"I told her everything that had happened, but I did not complain about Mrs. Flynn."

"You rather admired Mrs. Flynn?"

"I did not admire her, but I realised it was her duty."

Mr. Carrigan: "Do you say Kate Tobin is wrong when she swore here that in conversation with her you said that if Mrs. Flynn brought the priest to you twice she had two inquests in the house?"

Mary Cole: "I never used that expression and never thought it. I am positive on that."

She was next closely questioned on the point as to which field she found the cow on the evening of July 27th. She was mistaken in her first statement that she found her on the schoolhouse side of the road.

The witnesses, John Hennessey and Mary Bostic, were mistaken when they swore that they saw her driving the cow in the field on the other side where Philomena was drowned.

"When John Hennessey thought that he saw you in the field with a child wearing a red coat his eyes were deceiving him?"

"It is possible."

"On July 27th, Mrs. Flynn was upstairs resting and Mr. Flynn was away at the Rathdowney Show and you did not expect him back?"

"I did, because he was to come home in the afternoon."

"Was he at school that day?"

"He was for a while, up to 11:00 a.m.."

"When Mrs. Flynn was upstairs, you went out for the cow.

Didn't you know it was the rule that you were not to leave the children by themselves?"

"That was only when there was no one in the house but myself."

Mr. Carrigan: "I put it to you that when you got her upstairs you went for the cow, and then concealed from her that you had brought the cow home?"

Mary Cole: "I did not conceal it. She did not ask me about the cow, and if she did I did not hear her, because I was busy with the baby."

In reply to further questions she denied having told Mr. Flynn that she had to go up to the end of the field to find the cow. She did not remember him asking her, and if he had she would have told him where she did find it."

"Miss Murray says you found the cow in the ferns at the end of the field?"

"I don't recollect ever telling her that; she must be making a mistake."

"And Mr. Flynn's making a mistake?"

"He is not telling the truth."

"Philomena was found drowned, and nobody thought of blaming you?"

"No."

"And on August 22nd you saw Maureen up to the time you left for the cow?"

"Yes."

"And you last saw her alive as she went to the door?"

"Yes."

"Do you say the child was strong enough to climb the fence and cross the field and fall into the river?"

"I could not say, I don't know what way she went."

"Do you say that on the previous occasion on which the child was found in the field the child climbed the fence?"

"She must have."

"At one time did you make the case that John Gorman was ahead of you when you were both searching?"

"I think I was ahead of Gorman."

"And you saw what he says he could scarcely see, something white in the water?"

"Yes, I called to him, and he jumped across to my side."

When further questioned she stated it surprised her that a child of seven years had been drowned in eight inches of water.

Mr. Carrigan: "Someone must have held these little children down in the water seven inches deep?"

Mary Cole: "I don't know."

This ended the cross-examination which had lasted for more than one hour.

Mrs. Margaret Carey, postmistress, gave evidence that on more than one occasion the Flynn children came along the road with other children as far as her house.

Timothy Bergin who stated that he has seven children, said that sometime before the drowning of the children, the little girl, Patricia Flynn, came in by herself to his house and asked for a drink of water. She looked to be about three years old. The incident came to his mind when he heard of the loss of the first child.

Mr. Justice O'Byrne: "Did you ever hear of a child of one year and ten months starting out by herself over country and crossing fences?"

"No, my Lord."

Miss Kathleen Murphy, Rushin, Mountrath, who employed Mary Cole up to the time of her arrest, stated that the Guards called for Mary several times, always about 6 p.m., and took her to the barracks a mile away.

On one occasion they did not bring her back until 10:00 p.m. and on another it was 12:00 midnight.

The Court adjourned to Friday March 23, 1928.

CHAPTER SEVENTEEN

WITNESSES RECALLED

☙

After the close of the case for the Defence, His Lordship was handed down a list of questions upon which the Jury asked for enlightenment. He stated to the jury that the questions which they had written down would necessitate recalling some of the witnesses which His Lordship proceeded to do.

He recalled Mrs. Flynn, who, in reply to his questions, stated that at no time did she give the red coat to the accused to be washed.

His Lordship: "Can you tell us definitely that you did not give it to her to be washed on the 27th July?"

"I think not. I did not."

"Were any clothes washed that day —a Wednesday?"

"There was some washing done on Monday and Tuesday and Wednesday—some small things."

"Where were they put to dry?"

"In the back yard."

"Did you see the clothes hanging up there?"

"I recollect seeing the clothes on the line on the day of the inquest, that was Thursday."

"Was the little red coat amongst them?"

"I cannot recollect seeing it."

"It may have been there?"

"It may. I do not recollect seeing it."

With regard to the incident of the child Philomena being found in the field on July 15th, his Lordship asked Mrs. Flynn did she say to Mary Cole when she heard about it: 'We will have to watch Phil from this out.' The witness replied that she was almost certain she made use of the remark.

John Hennessey, recalled, told his Lordship that the child that he saw in the field with the master's maid was a very small child, in his mind not more than two years old. He was positive that was the day Philomena was drowned, because it was the only day about that time that he had his mother with him in Phelan's shop.

Other of the witnesses were recalled and further questioned by the judge on points of their evidence.

The boy, John Tynan, explained that when he was cycling down the road on the evening of 22nd of August he saw the child Maureen on the road before he saw Mary Cole coming out of Mr. Flynn's yard gate. He saw the child at the gate leading into Mr. Flynn's field. She had passed out of his view when he saw Mary Cole.

Dr. McCarthy explained to his Lordship that the bruise he saw on Philomena's forehead was caused while the blood was still in a state of circulation, or, rather, fluidity.

CHAPTER EIGHTEEN

MARCH 23, 1928
MR. WALSH ADDRESSES
THE JURY

❧

Mr. Walsh, Counsel for the Defence, opened his address to the jury on Friday, March 23rd at 11:35 a.m..

He said that before he directed the attention of the jury to the evidence that had been adduced, in that great trial in the last three days, he wished to call their attention to a most important and, he might say, almost iniquitous matter in connection with that case. Mr. Carrigan, the senior state prosecutor, stood up there and with all the astuteness that marked him as a great advocate, held up to them a picture of a terribly dramatic and sensational double murder. That was an exaggerated picture. Mr. Carrigan had told them that they must blot out of their minds their knowledge of juvenile crime. "He would, if he could, denude you of your common-sense," remarked counsel. Mr. Carrigan had painted for them a picture of a sorrowing mother.

"Well," said counsel, "while my sympathies go out to every father and mother who lose their children in any circumstance, and especially in these circumstances, where two little girls were brought in dead from the river, very little of my sympathy goes out to Mrs. Flynn."

Mr. Carrigan, in order to attract their sympathy from the very start, told them how the sorrowing mother took her other children and left the scene of her grief for a time.

"He tells you that poor people like the Flynns have to push and strive, but what are the real facts? Mrs. Flynn and her husband were in receipt of £550 a year as National Teachers. They had, in addition, a farm of thirty acres and stock. They also had a motor car." Counsel proceeded, "these are the poor people, according to Mr. Carrigan, who can afford only one servant, Mary Cole, who was the absolute slave in this household."

Going through the evidence analytically, counsel drew

attention to the remarkable discrepancies which marked the evidence of the witnesses for the State, especially with regard to the question of the red coat and the times at which it was sought to prove that Mary Cole was seen in the field, either alone or with one of the children. Mr. Carrigan would have them believe that the trip to Tramore was brought about as the result of the feelings of a sorrowing mother. But it turned out that this visit to Tramore had been arranged long before the drowning of the children. As to the likelihood of a child passing to the river close by the stump of the tree that had been referred to so much, they all knew that there was nothing unlikely in it, especially in the case of children accustomed from day to day to play in the fields and not always accompanied.

He asked them to discount the evidence of the girl, Kate Murray, who said that from the kitchen she saw the accused passing at the window at the time that Maureen was missing. This evidence, like so much of the evidence in the trial, was the outcome of a fantastic imagination. So far as Kate Murray's testimony was concerned, it could not weigh against the accused, and in the case of John Tynan, which had been relied on, he contended that the jury would have perceived that the most that he could say was that he saw Mary Cole and Maureen at really different times, and that when he saw Mary Cole, the child had already disappeared.

Dealing with the evidence of Michael Flynn, the father, it would have been noted that the bank of the river had been eaten away by the flow of the water, and that was a most important thing to remember. It showed that the old ordnance survey map could not be relied upon as a faithful indication of the conditions which prevailed at the time of these events.

It was up to the State to prove their case up to the hilt, and that they had certainly not done. Counsel said that he took upon himself the responsibility of putting his client in the box, and of giving the jury the advantage of her own statement. Upon her evidence he confidently relied as establishing a complete and impressive answer to the circumstances as put forward by the State. That young girl was subjected to a long, and trying, and searching cross-examination by Mr. Carrigan, and certainly he did not 'catch her out'. No, she answered fully, candidly, and unhesitatingly every query put to her.

There was not a scintilla of difference in the story told by her all along, from the inquest to her appearance in the witness chair of that Court. From six o'clock to ten on one night and from six to midnight on another she was examined and cross-examined by the Superintendent of Police and that at a time when she never anticipated that she would be arrested. It staggered Mr. Carrigan that she never varied in her statements. She could not vary because she was telling the simple truth. In the witness chair she did not accuse anyone of making up a case against her. She simply said that they were making a mistake.

It was plain that Hennessey, who often went to Phelan's, was mistaken as to the day that he saw Mary Cole and the child with the red coat in the field. He would not insult the intelligence of the jury by going into the fantastic stories about fairies and ghosts introduced by the prosecution. Even if Mary Cole said anything of the kind, what more could it be than childish gossip? The jury had it put to them by Mr. Carrigan that that fifteen-year-old girl had a monster mind. That was the only explanation that he could give for her telling the simple truth as she knew it. They themselves, must have come to the opinion, after seeing her and hearing her, that if any one of the witnesses in the case gave his or her evidence more straightforwardly than another, that one was the accused. That girl of fifteen, whose whole future was in their hands, did not yet fully realise the effect of an adverse verdict. Sorrow had come into the home of Mr. and Mrs. Flynn when their children were taken from them, but the parting of a mother with her convict daughter, her first born child, was a greater sorrow. In death there was no dishonour.

Before the jury came to the conclusion to part this mother and daughter in the disgrace of a convict, they must be satisfied beyond yea or nay that the State had established their case. The facts did not justify them in coming to any conclusion, but the one — that Mary Cole was not guilty.

Counsel spoke for five minutes less than an hour. When towards the end he referred to her mother, the girl in the dock broke down for the first time in the four days of the trial, and wept silently.

CHAPTER NINETEEN

MR. CARRIGAN RESPONDS FOR THE STATE

≈

Mr. Carrigan, replying for the prosecution, said that were he in Mr. Walsh's place he would have difficulty in addressing the jury with such adroitness and such brevity, leaving them to understand at the conclusion of his very dexterous address that there was not much to be said about this case more than he had suggested rather than said to them. He (Mr. Carrigan) did not claim to deserve either the compliments or—in this particular case the animadversions of counsel for the defence. His duty was simply to lay the facts before them, and it concerned him just as much and just as little as any member of the public what the jury's verdict might be, if it was a verdict arrived at in accordance with the evidence. He thought that the jury must come to the conclusion that murder had been done. Somebody had committed murder. If they came to that conclusion, then he thought the way was clear for them to follow, to find that the person who committed the double murder was in the dock.

Referring to the drowning of Philomena, counsel said that here was a little toddler, who must have escaped observation, left the prisoner who was in charge of her, traveled along the road unnoticed, clambered over a fence, gone through a field, over rough ground and fallen into the river. He suggested strongly that that child could not have drowned itself but must have been willfully drowned. Maureen, who had reached the use of reason, was found in a place to which she could have gone herself, but drowned in eight inches of water.

Who was the somebody who could have a motive in destroying these children? They had heard of Jack the Ripper, who for the lust of murder took the lives of innocents. But they had there a body of evidence, including the girl's own evidence, that she had a grievance, a bitter rankling against Mrs. Flynn, who exposed her relations with these boys and called in the Parish Priest. "This phenomenal juvenile criminal, untaught and without experience," proceeded counsel, "presents to you the case of a girl who looks a woman in appearance and has a mind more powerful and more agile, and imagination than any of you could come across in the experience of a lifetime." Yesterday they had heard her state coolly in the witness chair that she realised that it was Mrs. Flynn's duty to speak to the priest about her conduct. One would think that it was a headmistress in an advanced school or the head of a community of sisters, with education, training and experience of life who sat in the witness chair yesterday.

Every witness in the case must, according to the defence, have either told untruths or greatly exaggerated. But not a witness was produced on behalf of the accused to support her own account of her movements. On her own confession, she succeeded in the presence of her master, mistress and Parish Priest, in denying the charges made against her.

The jury would have noticed that she gave her evidence with a cleverness and coolness that was phenomenal and unnatural. One who, with little education, without having ever, perhaps, seen a cinema show, faced a lengthened cross-examination with almost miraculous equanimity. They were dealing with a juvenile of portentous monstrosity; for if they held that drowning had been done, then there was no one who could be charged with it but the girl in the dock, and she did it with supernatural cleverness and ingenuity.

Everybody concerned with the case had been deceived by this extraordinary girl, and, as to her statements made and signed by her they could only be described as most extraordinary intellectual achievements, by which after an interval she repeated her versions with no variations, save one, and that of little or no importance. She showed a superhuman power, that without knowledge or experience, displayed an ability such as one would be expected from one with a college or university education, and of masterful capacity.

She was, he said, extremely clever but she made two fatal slips, and those were when she willfully misplaced the position in the fields where she found the cow on each of the two occasions. Somebody placed the sturdy Maureen in the water and held her there until she became unconscious. Nobody had a motive for doing so except the accused.

Mr. Carrigan ended his address at 1:40 p.m., then Court adjourned for lunch and resumed at 2:25 p.m..

Immediately after lunch Mr. Justice O'Byrne commenced the summation of the case for the jury.

CHAPTER TWENTY

MARCH 23, 1928 2:35 P.M. MR. JUSTICE O'BYRNE'S CHARGE TO THE JURY

&

Mr. Justice O'Byrne in addressing the Jury said:

"Gentlemen of the Jury, you have followed this case with great care and attention for the past five days and I have excellent reasons for knowing that you have followed with the most careful scrutiny every phase of the evidence that has been produced before you. That relieves me of a great deal of responsibility and it simplifies very much the task which I have to perform in charging you at the end of the case. My duty is also relieved to a considerable extent by the very careful way in which the evidence has been analysed by Counsel on behalf of the prosecution and on behalf of the defence respectively. Mr. Walsh has said to you everything that could be said on behalf of his client and Mr. Carrigan very seldom leaves anything unsaid on behalf of the prosecution.

There was just one phrase in the address of Mr. Carrigan to which I take exception. In the course of his address he referred to the accused as 'a youthful criminal.' That term was misused and misapplied. The girl in the dock is, in the eyes of the law, innocent. She is presumed to be innocent until she is proved to be guilty and you must regard her as being innocent unless and until you are satisfied by the evidence that she is guilty of one or other of the crimes which you are investigating. You may not act upon suspicion. You may only act upon proof and the proof which you require is proof which will bring home to you, human certainty of the guilt of the accused. In the course of your deliberations you will, as you are bound to do, give to the accused the benefit of any reasonable doubt which you may have as to her guilt and she is entitled to the benefit of that doubt upon each issue which you have to try and determine.

I don't desire in this case that you should have any

misconception as to the meaning of reasonable doubt.

That term is usually heard of in connection with criminal trials and as you all know every person who is being tried is entitled to the benefit of that doubt. Now, a Jury in trying a criminal case can and must only act on the evidence produced before them. A criminal trial is one of the affairs of life, which must be dealt with by human beings, and it is not necessarily required in a criminal trial that the Jury should have that kind of certainty which is referred to as metaphysical or mathematical certainty. That is not required nor is it humanly possible to have it. You can have human certainty—that is the certainty which you recognize and act upon in your own affairs of life not in the trivial or commonplace affairs but in the important affairs of life, then you will give the accused the benefit of any such doubt. That is the kind of doubt which we refer to in law as a reasonable doubt—the kind of doubt which a reasonable man of the world would recognize and act upon in his own affairs of life.

Now having said so much we approach the consideration of the facts of this case and it is preeminently a case for a Jury. The issues which are involved are substantially issues of fact. In the course of my address I shall probably have occasion to make observations on various matters including the credibility of witnesses when and in so far as I state my views. But on questions of fact on my own view of the facts and of the inferences to be drawn from the facts, I desire you at the outset to understand that I do it entirely for your guidance and assistance without wishing in any way to impose on you my own views of the facts. I must not do so because you gentlemen, are the sole judges of fact—you are the sole judges as to the credibility of the witnesses—you are the sole judges of the issues of fact which are involved in the case and of all the inferences of fact to be drawn. You are not bound by any observations which I may make to you upon these questions and as I told you these observations are being made entirely for your assistance and for that purpose only.

Now, in this case there are four important dates to be remembered. These are of course the two dates—the 27th of July and 22nd of August on which these two children were found drowned. There are two other dates of some importance, the 30th of June and 15th of July and I shall approach these dates and deal with them in chronological order.

Now, in the indictment before you, and in the Counts that you are investigating, the accused is charged with the willful murder of the two infant children and in both cases the same issues are involved. In each case you will have to determine, in the first instance whether or not a particular child died accidentally or by human agency. If in either case, you come to the conclusion that the child died by accident then the accused will be entitled to an acquittal in respect of that child. If in either case, you come to the conclusion that the child didn't die by accident but by human agency then you must go further and determine whether or not the accused girl was the person through whose instrumentality that child met its death.

Now, in the month of June of last year, a rather unpleasant incident happened. It was reported to Mr. and Mrs. Flynn that this girl had been out at night with some boys from the neighbourhood and you will remember in a general way the evidence of Mrs. Flynn with reference to that occurrence. I don't intend to refer you in detail to that evidence but a meeting was arranged in the house of the Flynns at which on the first occasion Mr. and Mrs. Flynn and the accused girl, the Parish Priest, and some boys from the neighbourhood were present and the accused was taxed with this incident. She denied it— denied it very strenuously—and when the meeting broke up it was arranged that a further meeting should take place on the following night and that some other boys should be present. That first meeting according to the evidence took place on or about 30th of June. On the following night, the Parish Priest again attended. There were some other boys present. Mr. Flynn was there. The accused girl was inside in the kitchen and when these various persons had assembled Mrs. Flynn went in to her and implored her to confess so as to avoid the necessity of having this kind of inquiry in the presence of these men and she thereupon admitted that she had been out on this particular night.

Now gentlemen, you are only concerned to a very limited extent with that occurrence. We are not considering or attempting to determine any question of guilt on the part of Mary Cole with reference to the occurrence that was dealt with at this interview. The only way in which these events are evidence at all is, in so far as they might satisfy you as to the state of mind of Mary Cole, and as to her attitude towards the Flynns and particularly towards Mrs. Flynn. They are relied upon by the State as constituting a motive for these crimes which the State allege were committed by Mary Cole. That is the only way in which they ought to be considered by you.

Now, what was the state of mind of Mary Cole after these incidents? It is quite possible that you will come to the conclusion that in connection with these incidents, Mrs. Flynn was not as kind or as sympathetic as she might have been towards Mary Cole. You may think that she went a bit too far—that she went too far in taking away from Mary Cole this costume which she had given her—that she went too far during the fortnight subsequent to this incident in referring time after time to this incident. It is quite possible you will take that view. It seems to be a reasonable view and on that account it should be considered by you but only in so far as it informs your minds of the condition of Mary Cole's mind immediately after that incident and prior to the drowning of these two children.

Mary Cole herself says that all the unpleasantness blew over in the course of a fortnight. She says in her evidence: 'Mrs. Flynn took the costume from me. I didn't mind very much—I was ashamed and sorry.' She was not really cold after this. She was not really friendly. I tried to please her in every way. After the fortnight this unpleasantness blew over. This was the middle of July and I was as friendly with her as ever.

Now that is her evidence—that a fortnight before one of these children was drowned the unpleasantness had passed and she was as friendly as ever with Mrs. Flynn. Gentlemen, do you accept that? Do you accept that as true and accurate evidence as to the state of Mary Cole's mind in or about the middle of July? It is an important element in this case. You have the evidence of Mrs. Flynn, that she was never, after this incident, quite so satisfactory as she had been previously. She says she was silent, that during the fortnight immediately subsequent to that incident, she appeared to Mrs. Flynn not to have her mind on her work, and she said she (Mrs. Flynn) had occasion to refer to this incident and tell the girl that she couldn't have her mind on her work when she had it on other things.

You have the evidence of Kate Tobin and I don't think it can seriously be suggested to you in connection with her evidence that Kate Tobin was telling you what she knew to be untrue. That of course is a matter for you and not for me but it seems to me that no reason—no real reason—was suggested why Kate Tobin should come up to give you an untrue account of her conversation with the accused. Now what does she tell you? She said that she remembered this conversation taking place long afterwards. It took place after both these children had been drowned. 'She (that is, Mary Cole) said to me that Mrs. Flynn had been very hard to give her a costume and then take it away' and then she added 'she also said that if Mrs. Flynn had brought the priest to her twice that she had two inquests in the house since.'

Now gentlemen, consider that for a moment. Consider first whether that incident took place. Kate Tobin tells you it did, and it is not the kind of incident about which she could really make a mistake. It is too unusual for any witness to make a mistake about it, but secondly, in considering that incident, what you will have to consider is the credibility of Kate Tobin on the one hand and Mary Cole on the other. Mary Cole says she never said such a thing and Kate Tobin said she did and you must determine between them which of them you believe. If you accept the evidence of Kate Tobin as being true evidence and as being accurate evidence and if you find as a fact that at this time after these two children had been drowned, Mary Cole made use of the expression that 'if Mrs. Flynn had brought the priest to her twice she had two inquests in the house since'—then what opinion will you form as to the mental condition of the accused Mary Cole, a girl of fifteen and a half years of age, a girl who had been living in the house of the Flynns for in or about a year and during that period had been looking after, nursing and feeding these children—children of whom she says herself she had been very fond? Whether she had any part in the killing of these children or not, one would expect that with her opportunities of being with these children and she being as she says herself very fond of them herself, she would have been so shocked by this double occurrence as at any rate to have the greatest sympathy and sorrow for the Flynn family.

That is what you would expect from any normal being

especially from any girl of fifteen years who for a period of one year had these children under her care and control, nursing them and feeding them and looking after them day after day. It is a shock to any reasonable human being that such a statement should have been made. In addition to that we have the evidence of Kate Murray and again in her case it is difficult to see what object she could possibly have in coming up and telling you an untrue story. She came to this household in the early days of August when Mrs. Flynn with three of the children was away in Tramore and she told you that during the interval when Mrs. Flynn was away—and this was after one of the children had been drowned and prior to the drowning of the second, she says that Mary Cole made complaints to her about Mrs. Flynn. She complained about her calling in the priest and exposing her [Mary Cole] and taking away her character. She [Mary Cole] said she thought she had been greatly wronged and Kate Murray says she made that complaint several times.

Do you believe that these incidents took place in the early part of August of last year, after Philomena had been drowned and before Maureen had been drowned? Now again that is denied by Mary Cole and again you must come to a conclusion as to which of these witnesses you will believe. If you are satisfied that the story told by Kate Tobin was true that the accused made use of these extraordinary expressions about Mrs. Flynn having had two inquests in the family, if you believe the story of Kate Murray that during that month of August the accused frequently complained of the action of Mrs. Flynn towards her, then you will probably be satisfied that not only prior to the drowning of Philomena but even after that, that the accused had been nursing ill will against Mrs. Flynn and had a grudge against her. What is the attitude of mind suggested by these statements which Kate Murray and Kate Tobin allege were used to them? Now, the mental attitude of the accused towards the Flynns is a matter of supreme importance. It is a matter of supreme importance when you come to consider the events of the 27th of July and the 22nd of August. The case for the prosecution here is that at that time the accused was actuated by feelings of malice, ill will and hatred towards Mrs. Flynn and the Flynn family and that she wreaked her vengeance on the two innocent children.

The next date I have to deal with is the 15th of July and the events of that date are solely concerned with Philomena who was actually drowned twelve days later—on the 27th of July. Apart from this occasion it is not suggested that this little child Philomena, a child of one year and ten months of age, ever wandered away from home. She did go about the roads sometimes with the other children as one would expect but apart from that it is not suggested that on any other occasion did she wander away from home alone. On this occasion, it is alleged by the accused that she did wander away by herself and that by herself she found her way into this field at the end of which she was drowned some twelve days later. The accused gives an account of that incident and this is her account. She says, 'I remember one occasion on which I found the cow on the right hand side of the road and on the left bank of the river.' That would be down here in the direction in which Philomena was subsequently drowned (indicated on the map.) She continues and says, 'on this occasion, when I was driving the cattle towards the road, I saw Brophy. I did not see any of the children up to that. Later, when at the gate I looked back and saw Philomena going down through the fields. This was before I spoke to Brophy.' Now that is a matter of importance when I come to refer you to his evidence. She says, 'This was before I had spoken to Brophy. He spoke to me. He said, 'Good evening.' I suddenly saw the child going down the field beside the shed. Brophy said 'the young villain must have followed you.' I think he added he saw the child going down the field when passing by. He had got off his bicycle. I took the child home. When I took the child home I told Mrs. Flynn. I asked her if she had not missed the child and she said 'No.' Then I told her where I found her. She said, 'We will have to mind Phil from this out.'

This was a fortnight before July 27th.

Now that is the account of Mary Cole and it suggests that as she was coming up the field she saw the child. She saw Brophy. She saw the child before she had spoken to Brophy, that the child had wandered after her that it started to wander down the field and that when she went back she told Mrs. Flynn where she found the child. Now neither Mrs. Flynn's account nor Brophy's account quite coincides with that of Mary Cole. Mrs. Flynn says, 'The children never strayed away a long distance from the house. The accused told me she had found Phil some distance from the house. This was on the 15th July. She went on to say that when returning with the cow she stood. She says, 'She looked in and saw the child going straight down the field. She said she had come out of the field herself. I said, 'How is it you did not see her' and she said, 'She must have gone in at the shed when I was coming up.' I said she could not get in and I told Mary Cole that and Mary Cole answered, 'Well she was going down the field anyway', and then Mrs. Flynn goes on to say, 'On the Saturday after Philomena's death I questioned her again and said, 'On the evening she was down the field what direction was she going?' and she said, 'She was going straight down the river.' I said, 'My God, why didn't you tell me that,' and she said she had been going in the direction of the spot where she had been found.'

That was on the Saturday after the little girl was drowned and the accused said to Mrs. Flynn she had been going in the direction of the part where she was found. Now Brophy's account is of such importance in connection with this incident, which is so very vital in considering what took place on the 27th July, that I have gone to the trouble of getting from the Official Stenographer a complete transcript of his evidence and I shall read the whole of it for you:

"Mr. Carrigan: 'Do you remember an evening previously seeing the little child Philomena?'

'Yes Sir'

'How long before the child was drowned?'

'About ten days.'

'Under what circumstances did you come across her?'

'I was cycling in the direction of Longford Cross from the priest's house about 6 o'clock, and when I came to the Flynn's shed I heard a child crying. I got off my bicycle and stood up on the ditch and Philomena was standing inside in the field crying.'

'How high is the ditch there?'

'About two and a half feet from the road side.'

'And from the Flynn's side?'

'About 5 feet.'

'Where was the child?'

'She was standing right under the ditch Sir, crying.'

'In distress?'

'Yes'

'And what did you do?'

'I stood talking to the child for a minute or two pacifying her.'

'Did you see anyone?'

'Yes, I saw Mary Cole. She was coming up the field with the cow.'

'And did you watch as she came along?'

'Yes Sir.'

'And when she came near what did you do?'

'I called her and told her that Philomena was at the shed and to bring her home.'

'And you brought the child out of the field—what did you do? Mary Cole went back into the field for the child.'

'Did she come up the field?'

'Yes she came in the direction of the gate and I told her and she went in the direction of the child.'

'Did you go to the gate?'

'Yes it was only a matter of a second to get there. The gate was closed.'

'And did you or Mary Cole open the gate?'

'No Mary Cole opened the gate.'

'Is that the only occasion you ever saw this little child astray?'

'That is all.'

'Would it have been possible for that child, knowing her as you did, to get into the spot in the field over the fence?'

'Mr. Justice O'Byrne: I think that is a matter for the Jury.'

'Mr. Carrigan: Describe that spot—is it where the old stump of the tree is, that had fallen?'

'Mr. Walsh: What is the number of the photograph?'

'Mr. Carrigan: 'No. 11.' (To witness) 'do you recognise that photograph: is that where you saw the child crying?'

'Yes Sir.'

'Mr. Justice O'Byrne: 'Just point out where?'

'Witness: 'Right under the shed opposite the old stump.'

'Mr. Justice O'Byrne: 'At the left hand side of the shed?'

'No, the right hand side.'

'Mr. Justice O'Byrne: 'Take a pen and put an X on the spot on the photograph where you saw her.' Witness did so.'

'Mr. Justice O'Byrne (to the Jury): 'It is there gentlemen on the extreme left of the shed.' (To witness) 'Is this the old stump you refer to?'

'Yes My Lord, the back of the shed is on the right.'

'Is the stump you refer to higher than the shed?'

'No my Lord.'

'Where is the stump there?'

Witness: 'I made a mistake about that.'

'Are you able to see it there?'

'I don't quite understand the photograph my Lord.'

'Mr. Carrigan: 'I will withdraw the photograph.'

[CROSS-EXAMINATION BY MR. WALSH]

'You say you know this place very well?'

'Yes.'

'And the stump of the tree that we heard so much about is on the road?'

'No it is on the ditch.'

'The ditch adjoining the road in which you saw the child?'

'Yes sir.'

'Do you know the gate on the road to that field by Longford Cross?'

'Yes I do.'

'And do you know the road I think it goes to Delora Bridge, to the road along Longford Cross?'

'Yes.'

'Would I be right in saying that the fence immediately around the corner is very low?'

'Oh it is not very low.'

'Much lower than the fence along the road between the Bridge and Longford Cross?'.

'Well it is lower.'

'Lower I think than in the spot in the fence between the

Bridge and Longford Cross?'

'Oh I would not say it is altogether but it is lower.'

'Now when you heard this little child crying on that evening—the child you told us about discovering, she was just inside the fence?'

'Yes Sir.'

'And you told us that Mary Cole was away down the field somewhere?'

'I saw her coming up the field after a couple of minutes.'

'So actually when you heard the child crying and got on the fence to see where the cries were coming from Mary Cole was not then in sight?'

'No sir.'

'So that wherever Mary Cole was then she must have been at the extreme end of the field at the other side?'

'She couldn't have been more than 200 yards away.'

'Was she then coming towards the gate?'

'Yes.'

'And it was about 2 minutes from the time you saw the child?'

'Yes. I was pacifying the child for a minute or two.'

'And after the lapse of a minute or 2 you saw Mary Cole 200 yards away?'

'Yes.'

'From where you saw her at the time you saw her, she must have been proceeding towards you before she came into your sight?'

'She was.'

'And she was turning the cow with her?'

'Yes.'

'Was she surprised or did she appear to be surprised when she came up and found the child there?'

'No, not a bit Sir.'

'And she took the child off home?'

'I told her to go back with the child and she went back with it.' ".

You will remember the incident of his [Thomas Brophy] being handed the photograph. He had some difficulty in finding the exact place. He pointed to one place in the first instance and afterwards he said he made a mistake.

He was cross-examined by Mr. Walsh who asked him 'Was she surprised or did she appear surprised when she came up and found the child there and the answer was 'No, not a bit Sir.'

This seems to be of importance. She was not a bit surprised. Now the account of Mary Cole is shortly that at some stage whether as she was about to come on the road or as it appears to be more likely, from her words, when she was on the road she saw the child going down the field, and in the statement which Mrs. Flynn says she made to her on the Saturday after the child's death, she said that she saw her coming down the fields in the direction of the very spot where she was subsequently found drowned.

Does that in your opinion agree with the evidence of Brophy? Take the evidence of Brophy if you believe it. Do you think that the child wandered down through the land and cross over into the field alone or does it rather suggest to you that Mary Cole, the accused, had brought the child down, had left it where Brophy found it and had then gone off for the cow?

That would seem to explain the distress of the child, the child crying when Brophy came down. Brophy had a bicycle and he remained a minute or two pacifying it. He saw Mary Cole and he told her to take away the child and she took it back home.

You will remember in considering the case of this child, Philomena, that she was one year and ten months, a very young child, a child at an age when a lot of children have only been walking for a comparatively short time and when they are not too sure of their feet and when you would not expect them to go climbing fences.

The evidence of Brophy, if you accept it, does not suggest that the child had gone down there, cross the fence and made her way down the fields in the direction of the place where she was subsequently drowned. It seems to me, and again I tell you it is a matter for you rather than for me, it seems to suggest that the child had been left there and having been left there commenced to cry. She certainly, according to Brophy's evidence, was in the field when he saw her not going down the field, she was standing right inside the fence.

That brings us to the 27th of July the day when this little child was drowned.

I shall refer you to portions of the evidence of some witnesses as material for this particular purpose, and in dealing with the deaths of Philomena and Maureen I intend to segregate the evidence and refer you in the case of Philomena to the evidence dealing with that particular child, and in the case of Maureen, to the evidence relating to her case, you will have to consider these two separately and independently.

Now on the 27th of July, Mr. Flynn, the father, had been in school up to 11 o'clock. He then went to the Rathdowney Show and did not return home until 10 o'clock at night, hours after the child was drowned. Mrs. Flynn had been in her school. She had been home for lunch about 12:30. She went back to school and finally got home about 3:20 in the afternoon.

Three of the children had been in school for portions of the day, the three eldest children, Maureen, Eilis and Pat. The other child had been at home. Mrs. Flynn came home at 3:30 p.m.. She had some dinner and some of the Flynn children had dinner. She did some things and finally went to her room about 4:30 p.m., lay down, went to sleep for some time, and didn't come down until the Angelus Bell was ringing.

She tells you that; 'on that day about 4:30 p.m. I went upstairs; Philomena was then sleeping in the kitchen. I remained upstairs until the Angelus Bell rang. I had been asleep. When I came down Mary Cole was near the staircase giving a bottle of milk to the baby, Michael. I ordered her to go for the cow and took the bottle from her.'

Now Mrs. Flynn is very clear in her evidence that at that time she told Mary Cole to go for the cow. It is quite clear from the evidence that the cow at that time had been brought home and put into the house.

Mary Cole says her mistress did nothing of the kind and said nothing to her about the cow and certainly it is not suggested that she told Mrs. Flynn that the cow had been brought home and was then in the house.

Mrs. Flynn goes on to say, 'She (Mary Cole) said she wanted feeding stuff for the calf. I gave her the money. I did not see Philomena after coming down. I did not ask the accused about her before she went out. The accused was outside and I heard her talking baby talk outside. She came in and I asked if Phil was with her and she said, 'No, is not that she in the window upstairs.' I sent her up to look and she searched the rooms upstairs and downstairs. I sent her to the back and I went to the front and met her in the yard. I asked her when she saw the child last. She said, 'She (meaning Phil) was there a few minutes ago.' I sent her to Tynan's and I went to Longford Cross. I looked into the fields and I saw no sign of the child. I returned and met the accused in the yard. I asked her again, when did she see the child last and she said she was there outside the door when she brought the cow. I then sent her to try the back of Father Walsh's house. This was the first time I heard she had brought in the cow.'

Later on she is questioned about this and she says, 'When I came down from the bedroom the evening Philomena was drowned, I understood the cow had not been brought in. I told Mary Cole to go for the cow and she said nothing. She had to go for foodstuff for the calf. I asked her either that evening or the following Saturday when she last saw Philomena and she said she was there when she was milking the cow, pointing to the right of the front door. I had already heard from her that she had brought in the cow but not that she had milked it'. Later on she is questioned again about this when she was re-examined by Mr. White, and she said that Mary Cole had said the child must have gone in at the shed. This was on the occasion of the 15th July. She said that fence at the shed was about two and a half feet high. You then get over the slippery surface of a tree and get down about 5 feet. Now, in answer to me, she said she went down to the field. You will remember shortly after the child was missed she went to the field and searched for the child. I asked her if the gate was fastened when she went down and she answered that it was fastened, that there was a fastening near the top and wire netting on the gate.

Now Gorman actually found the child and he gives the following account: He says he crossed the fence some place near the bridge and got in near the bank of the river, the left hand bank. He says, 'Going down I saw Mary Cole on the other side of the river. She was approaching the river. She was in the pasture field opposite the fence separating the oats field from the pasture field. She was going straight into the river. I was approaching and she said Phil was missing for an hour or an hour and a half and that she was afraid she was drowned'. Remember gentlemen, that this is the first child and before any drowning had taken place. She said, 'Phil was missing for an hour or an hour and a half and she was afraid she was drowned.' A very significant statement if it ever was made.

Continuing he said: 'She turned and went down the river and I asked her if she was down the river before and she said something I could not catch. She kept walking on the right bank. I was behind on the left bank. When we went about a hundred yards she called and said the child was in the water. She was 20 yards in front of me. I crossed the river. I jumped across and got to where the child was. She went within two or three yards of the child and stood. I did not know it was the child until I was within five or six yards of it. The accused kind of ran from the spot. I lifted the child out of the river. She was lying on her face. There was about 16 inches of water there and the body was covered by the water. She was completely submerged and there was three inches of water over the back of the child. The child was dead. She was dressed in a white dress. The accused stood. When I called her she did not come. She stood in her place. I had the child out. I rubbed her hands and I said 'there is no use, the child is dead. Mary Cole agreed. I carried the child to the house and she came with me.'

Now, in cross examination by Mr. Walsh, he was asked about this statement that Mary Cole made, the expression she used about the child being drowned, and he says it may be to the effect that 'it would be awful if it was drowned.'

He was questioned as to how the child could have got into the river and he says, 'I would say that the child should have entered from the right hand bank, that is from the side of the Hurling Field.'

You may remember he was questioned about the width of the river about that place and he says it was about four yards wide and the child was about three feet from the right bank.

Dr. Phelan's evidence is to the effect that he examined the child and said that in his opinion death was due to drowning. There was a discoloration of the skin on the right forehead and no other mark of violence and in answer to me he said he was unable to say if the mark was caused in the life time of the child or after its death.

Now we come to the evidence of one of the most important

witnesses in this branch of the case and that is the evidence of John Hennessy. I think when you consider the evidence of John Hennessy, Mary Bostick and Delaney, who apparently has been accepted as a credible witness by the defence, that you can have very little doubt but that Hennessy and Mary Bostick are talking about the evening of July 27th.

When you hear the evidence of these three witnesses and see how the evidence of each of them fits into the evidence of the others, I think you will be satisfied on that point.

You will remember in a general way that Hennessy says that some distance back from Longford Cross, about half a mile back, he passed Mary Bostick on the road. He came to Camross, put up the horse and accompanied his mother to the priest's house, and when he had finished in the priest's house, he came back and went into the shop and that Mary Cole was there then and he asked who she was.

Mary Cole is the girl he says he had already seen in the field and to whom he had referred as the 'Masters maid'. Mary Cole admittedly that evening went over from Flynn's house to that shop and taking the evidence of all these witnesses together I think it is a fact beyond all doubt that the evening that Mary Bostick and John Hennessy are talking about is the evening Philomena was drowned.

Hennessy says, 'I was going to Phelan's. I was driving a pony and trap. I passed Mary Bostick on the road. She was driving a donkey. She was way, probably less than a quarter of a mile, before I came to the Cross. At Longford Cross I saw the Master's maid and I took her to be driving out a cow. There was a little child with her. She was dressed in a red cloak.'

He was asked to whom he referred to as the Master, and he said: 'I refer to the School Master. I saw the Master's maid, there was a little child with her, she was dressed in a red cloak.' A little child not two years of age, according to his evidence this morning. I called him this morning and he said he is a married man and has children of his own and I asked him what age was this child and his words were 'I don't know. I don't think she was two years of age.'

Continuing, Hennessy said the coat was the colour of the coat produced in Court. 'The cow was there, and more cattle. I didn't know her then'. Apparently he knew she was the Master's maid. 'That is the girl in the dock. She was about six perches in the field. This was on the left hand side as I came up that way. About six perches down the field from the gate', and he said he was in the field afterwards with the police officer. 'I went to Phelan's yard; it is in front of the shop. My mother went to the Parish Priest's, he was not at home. I had some business in the shop. I was there, about half an hour altogether. While in the shop I saw the Master's maid come into the shop and get linseed meal. She left when she got it.'

The gateway from the road leading to where Philomena's body was found.
— *source: Trial Evidence 1928*

On this 27th July one child was drowned, and when Mrs. Flynn came down from the bedroom Mary Cole said she wanted food for the calf and she thereupon went to the shop and got linseed meal. In cross-examination he said 'I saw the girl and a little child in the field. They were coming towards the gate. They were driving the cow towards the gate. I wondered at the Master to have his child out on such a wet evening.' Now comment is made and properly made by Mr. Walsh on the fact that some of the evidence would suggest it was a fine day. But we have the evidence of Mary Cole herself that earlier in the day it had been wet and there had been thunder about 2 o'clock, and there had also been rain. She was asked if there had been rain at this time and she said 'No, but it was dark.' Whether it was raining at that time or not, that field along by the river in which there is heavy ground would at any rate in all probability be very wet and Hennessy may have been referring to that. However, that is his evidence. He says, 'I wondered at the Master having his child out on such a wet evening. I saw her in the shop afterward. I asked the shop man who she was. It might be a quarter past six o'clock when I got home and I heard before leaving that they were looking for the child. I heard of the death of the child the next day. It was 2 or 3 months afterwards when I was asked to make a statement. There is no doubt it was the same evening as I was in the shop, that I saw the girl. I am not mixing them up. I knew they were looking for the child before I left.'

Apart from his evidence as to whether he is in a position to recall the evening or not, I think you will be satisfied the evening is fixed beyond all question by the evidence of the other witnesses Mary Bostick, Delaney, Mrs. Flynn and the evidence of Mary Cole herself. Mary Bostick says this evening she was in Camross. She had an ass and cart and there was a small brother with her. She came to Longford Cross and then she stated, 'I didn't notice anyone in the field when I was going up. I went to Phelan's shop and got goods I stayed a few minutes in the shop and started for home.'

It is quite clear she came along that road there shortly after Hennessy and dealing with the evidence of these two witnesses, Mr. Walsh said to you, first they may be making a mistake about the date, but I think that is hardly possible. And he further went on to say that Hennessy must be making a mistake if Mary Bostick is right and the other way about—that if Mary Bostick is right, Hennessy cannot be correct. Now that is not so. Hennessy came up and saw Mary Cole and the child in the field. This girl Bostick came along and didn't see them. The evidence of both of these witnesses can stand together. Mary Cole may have been in the field and Mary Bostick not have seen her, or in the interval she may have got to some position in the field from which Mary Bostick couldn't see her but unless you reject the evidence of Hennessy, I think you will be satisfied that when he was passing by a short distance in front of Mary Bostick, there was the girl in the field, whom he described as the Master's maid; whom he subsequently saw in Phelan's shop and whom he recognised as the girl in the dock. He says she was in the field and had with her a little child in a red coat, a little child not more than 2 years of age.

Continuing, Mary Bostick says, 'I was about 10 minutes in the shop. I then started for home. When I got to Longford Cross, Mary Cole was driving a cow about nine or ten yards from the gate.'

The cow had not moved much in the interval. Hennessy says that when he passed, she was six perches from the gate. Mary Bostick, when she was passing back, said the cow was nine or ten yards from the gate. Now a considerable interval elapsed. Mary Bostick was behind Hennessy on the road. An interval elapsed between the time Hennessy passed and the time Mary Bostick came up. In one case, the interval would appear to be very short, because in one place I think she says that when she came about the Longford Cross, she could see Hennessy about the Bridge and in another place she said he was never more than a quarter of a mile from her. Some interval passed. She was in Phelan's shop. She has business there. She spent about ten minutes there. She went back and on her way back she saw Mary Cole in the field. She didn't see anybody else. Now here is what she says, 'She was driving a cow. I saw nobody with her. That was about a quarter to 6 o'clock. I went on my way home.' And she says, 'I heard the Angelus Bell when I was about a quarter of a mile from Longford Cross.'

Now times, when stated in terms of hours and minutes are not of very much importance, in this case. I think, because you would never expect these witnesses to be very accurate about time, when there was no particular reason for being accurate, but an event such as this would fix the time—and she says — when about quarter of a mile from Longford Cross she heard the Angelus Bell ring, and that was in or about the time Mrs. Flynn came down from upstairs in her house. She was cross examined about the distance she was behind Hennessy. She says, 'I was a quarter of a mile behind him—he was tying his horse. I met his mother coming out of the shop gate. I was in about ten minutes in the shop. On the way back I saw Mary Cole.' Then in answer to me she said, 'I saw Mary Cole through the bushes. I only noticed the cow. I didn't notice any other cattle.' You will remember Hennessy's evidence—he noticed other cattle—and when she was recalled by me this morning and asked if the child was there, she said it could be there but she didn't take any particular notice.

The evidence of Delaney is of some importance if not for any other reason than the reason that he fixes the date and also for another reason which I will comment on when I reach his evidence.

This man is an assistant in the shop near Flynn's house. He would know all about this occurrence and he would not make any mistake about it. He says, 'On the 29th July I was in the shop. I saw three of the children, Maureen and the others running up the road. They were going from Flynns and they passed the shop. This was about 5:30 old time. I was in the yard. They passed out of my sight up the road. I saw John Hennessy. He came from the direction of Longford Cross. He was driving a pony and trap. His mother was with him. The children had not come back in the meantime. I went into the shop.'

Now apart from the fixing of the date that is the incident which I have referred to as being an incident of some importance in the evidence of Delaney.

He was apparently out about the place for some time before Henessey came up, about ten minutes before that he saw three of the Flynn children, three of the eldest passed by and they had not passed back when Hennessy came up. Where was the other child? Where was the other child that had been, some hour previously, at any rate, when Mrs. Flynn went upstairs, under the control of Mary Cole.

The three eldest children passed up the road. Philomena is not with them. They are still up the road when Hennessy comes up. Where is Philomena? Hennessy, if you accept his evidence, probably satisfies you that she was in the field at the corner in which she was drowned, dressed in a red coat and in the company of Mary Cole, the girl in the dock.

Delaney goes on and says, 'Mary Bostick came in about two minutes afterwards. I attended to her and she left. Hennessy came in afterwards. He went to the priest's house with his mother and came back. Hennessy came in. He spent a considerable time outside. He went to Father Walsh's before he came in. While in the shop Mary Cole came in. She came up the road from Flynn's. She was there about

5:40 o'clock old time and purchased meal for the calf.'

Now that is the case for the prosecution in reference to this child. The case for the defence is made by the evidence of the accused herself. You will remember in addition to the accused the other witnesses called by the defence but I do not think any of them will be of any assistance to you. Miss Carey was called to say she knew the Flynn children. On some occasions they came to her place with other children and this happened more than once.

Timothy Bergin was called and he said on one occasion, the time of which he could not fix even approximately, it may be last year or not, but on some occasion one of the Flynn children came into this house and asked for a drink. He does not know which of them but thinks it was Pat. He says also that there were other children about and then you have the evidence of Miss Kathleen Murphy, the employer of the accused after she had left the Flynn household.

So that I do not think any of these three witnesses will be of very much assistance to you and I shall refer you to the evidence of the accused with reference to the incidents of the 27th July, the time that Philomena was drowned.

Mary Cole, the accused, tells you she had finished about 5 o'clock and went for the cow. All the children had gone in including Phil. 'The children were in the house when I went for the cow. I prepared feeding for the calf. Michael was asleep when I was going out. I found the cow on the school side of the road and on the far side of the river near Mrs. Burke's.'

Now I asked her about this and she said, 'when you came to Longford Cross you turned to the left to go to Mrs. Burke's' and at any rate Mary Cole is quite clear in her evidence that on this evening that Philomena was drowned, she got the cow on some portion of the land on the left hand side of the road on the far side of the river.

That is absolutely inconsistent with the evidence given you by Hennessy and Mary Bostick. Both say that they saw the accused down in this field on the right hand side of the road. They both saw the cow. One saw her with a little child and the other without a child.

Mary Cole goes on to say in her evidence, 'I came back with the cow and put her in the house. I drove the cow across the river and out through the gate at the school wall.'

Hennessy and Mary Bostick say she was driving the cow. Hennessy says she was six perches [33 yards] away when he saw her and Mary Bostick says nine or ten yards. Mary Cole says she found the cattle and drove them across the river and drove them out into the field beside the school wall.

Mary Cole goes on with her evidence and says, 'The baby was still sleeping when I returned. He wakened up a few minutes afterward and I gave him a drink. While I was giving him the drink, Mrs. Flynn came down. I did not know Mrs. Flynn was going upstairs to have a rest. Mrs. Flynn took the bottle and continued feeding the baby and I told her about messages from the shop.'

You will remember Mrs. Flynn's account is, she took the baby and told the girl to go for the cow and in reply Mary said she wanted feeding stuff for the calf. Mary Cole says she said nothing about going for the cow.

She says, 'I told her about the messages from the shop. When I mentioned the messages she said Maureen would get them. I told her what the messages were and she sent me.'

She was then questioned about the finding of the body and she said she searched through the oats and on her way back she saw John Gorman who was coming by the river. She says, 'I was in the Hurling Field at this time. He spoke to me. He asked me how long the child was missing. I do not remember what I said. He understood what I was searching for. I was in front of him. I continued down the river. When I came near the bank I saw a little child lying in the water partly covered with the water.'

Now according to the evidence of John Gorman, the child was completely submerged and there were three inches of water over the body.

She says, 'I shouted, the child is here. He jumped across the river. I ran away. I was terrified at seeing the child in the water. I ran out of sight. He called me and I went back. I didn't go the whole way to the child. I am quite clear as to where I found the cow that evening.'

Now that is really the whole of the evidence with reference to Philomena, all the material parts of it.

The case for the accused is that she was not near that spot that evening, that the child was not with her, that the child was in the house when she came back, that she got the cow here (indicated) and drove it across the river and out by the gate beside the school wall.

You have the evidence of other witnesses that they actually saw her on that evening, which I think is fixed beyond all question, they saw her in the field which leads to the river where Philomena was drowned, saw her with the cow, and saw her there, one of them saw her with a little child.

You have in addition to that evidence, the evidence of Delaney, who says that some ten minutes or so before Hennessy came up he saw three of the children pass by up the road. Philomena was not with them. They were still up the road when Hennessy came up. Philomena was not with the three children. Her mother was asleep, the baby boy of some months old was apparently asleep and unless Philomena was with Mary Cole, we know of no person with whom she could have been.

Now we come to the 22nd of August and Mrs. Flynn's account of the occurrences on the 22nd of August is as follows: 'It was raining in the morning and fine in the evening. I was in the kitchen with Kate Murray about 5:30 o'clock. The food was being prepared for the calf and the accused was outside the back door. I saw Maureen. She came into the kitchen and she stretched across me with something. I spoke to her. She passed me and ran out. I heard her stop going out. She made an exclamation as if calling somebody. I didn't see her again alive. She was running when leaving the kitchen. I next saw the accused when she was returning from Pratt's.'

You will remember that Mr. Flynn sent her to Pratt's and coming back from Pratt's she was met by Mrs. Flynn. Mrs. Flynn described the search and goes on to say, 'I didn't see her, Mary Cole, for about three quarters of an hour. When I came back Maureen was in the house lying on a mattress. I went to the place where Philomena was found. My husband followed me. When I came back my husband and Dooley were rubbing the child in the back room. She appeared to be dead.'

Mr. Flynn, the husband, tells you that he spent the day indoors. He says it was a wet day. He says he saw Mary Cole cross the yard. This was about twenty-five minutes past or half past five o'clock. 'She had a bucket in her hand. When she got on the road she turned about and looked towards Phelan's shop. She stopped there and turned about and went on down the road in the direction of the bridge. Sometime afterwards I heard Kate Murray say something. I remained in the parlour. There was about a quarter of an hour between the time Kate Murray said something and Mary Cole going out.'

ORDINANCE MAP DETAIL USED AT TRIAL

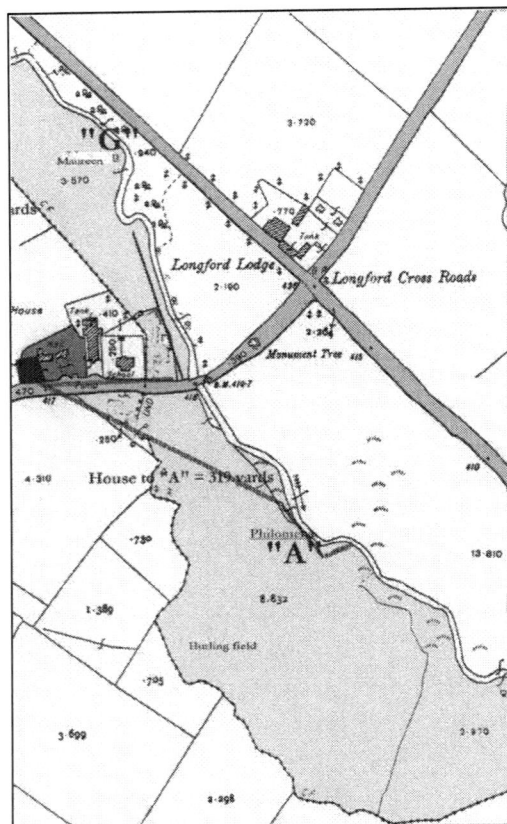

— *source: Trial Evidence 1928*

'I called the accused from the cow house. I told her to go and look for Maureen. I said, 'Go to Walsh's' and I returned to the gateway. Mary Cole was coming back on the road without the child and I called to her to go back and try Phelan's. I went through the fields towards "A (on the map)," the spot where Philomena was drowned. I returned to the road. I went up the right bank of the stream and I examined the field there. In the river I found Maureen. She was lying in the river at the point where it divides, "G (on the map)." She was lying on the right hand side, her head facing against the stream, her head inclined to the stream. She was on the right hand side, the face inclined to the front and turned downwards. The back of her head was up and body was lying in 8 or 9 inches of water. Part of the body was over the water. Her face was under the water. She was on the school side of the division of the stream. I carried her out and she was quite limp. There was froth on her mouth and she appeared to be dead. There was a mark on her forehead but I didn't observe it at first. I came back to the house and put her in bed in the accused's room. She was dressed but had no stockings or shoes on.'

I asked him later on if she was wearing stockings or shoes that day and he said she was not. Continuing, Mr. Flynn said, 'The mark was a black mark about the size of a penny and it was swollen. There is a sandy bed in the stream at point "G" on the map. Now he deals with a question which is of some importance. He says he spoke to Mary Cole that evening shortly afterwards. He says: 'I asked her where she got the cow and she said she got her at the farthest point of the land on the school side of the river.' Later on he was further questioned about this and he said that Mary Cole said that the cow was found at the far end of the field. I said 'Was it amongst the furze and she said 'Yes'. 'And the furze' he said, 'are here (indicated) in this little corner'. He (Flynn) said, 'There are scattered furze all over the place in that particular piece of land'. He says it was completely covered with furze and when he asked this girl was it amongst the furze she found the cow, she says it was.

Dr. McCarthy was brought to this child and he applied artificial respiration for some time. He found it was of no effect. He says he saw a mark on the forehead which was about the size of a shilling and had been caused in the lifetime of the child. It was a bruise and could be caused by coming in contact with some blunt object. Now Dr. McCarthy came back at his own request and he said about that mark that it may have been caused after unconsciousness but it was caused while the child was still alive, while the blood was still in circulation.

Now the little boy, John Tynan, a remarkably intelligent boy, gives evidence about seeing Mary Cole and Maureen this particular afternoon. There is some discrepancy between the evidence of Mary Cole on the one side and Mrs. Flynn on the other side as to what became of the child after she came into the scullery with the kettle but wherever she went it is clear from Tynan's evidence that within a few minutes afterwards she was out on the road going in the direction of this field, the field beside the school garden. He says, 'I remember this evening. I heard about the drowning as soon as the child was found. I saw Maureen that evening shortly before. She was in front of the school. She was coming from the direction of her own house. I saw Mary Cole at the same time she was coming out of Flynn's house. Maureen was then on the road. Mary Cole was carrying a bucket. I was on a bicycle. Maureen came from her own house. She was going in the same direction as Mary Cole, and then he says that he milked the cow the evening Philomena was drowned.

In cross-examination he says that it was nothing unusual to see Mary Cole with Maureen. 'I told the Guards about that a few months afterwards.' I recalled him this morning and he said in reply to me that when he saw Maureen she was in front of the school. 'When I came to Flynn's gate Mary Cole was coming out. Maureen had disappeared from view then. I didn't look into the field.'

You will remember this boy was going in the same direction as Maureen. He was on a bicycle. He was only a short distance away when he saw Maureen and when he came to Flynn's gate Mary Cole was going from the gate to the road. Maureen had disappeared and it is difficult to say where she could have gone save either into the school yard or into the field beside the school yard. She would probably have about time to get there. That she went into the fields is fairly certain because within a comparatively short time afterwards she was found drowned at the top of the field or half way up the field. Now you will remember Kate Tobin's evidence. She gave evidence as to statements which the accused made to her sometime after the death of both these children and she says that Mary Cole in referring to Maureen said, that 'she had left her at home'. She said she left her at home, 'because she was too fond of telling tales' She said that Maureen had asked her to let her go with her; that she went for the cow herself, that she came back and they started looking for Maureen, that she went searching and went to Miss Carey's and said to Miss Carey that Maureen must be drowned.

"That is what Mary Cole according to the evidence of Kate Tobin said to her, that shortly after this little child of almost seven years of age, within a few minutes after it had disappeared, she said to Miss Carey that she must be drowned. According to the evidence of Gorman when searching the field a few minutes after Philomena had disappeared she said to him, 'She must be drowned,' but in cross-examination Gorman admitted what she said might be, 'Would it not be an awful thing if she was drowned' and if you accept the evidence of Kate Tobin, if you accept it, she mentioned drowning in the case of Maureen to Miss Carey.

Now still following this conversation she said, 'Miss Carey said, Nonsense, a child like Maureen getting drowned.' A sensible remark, and a remark one would be inclined to make about a child of that age.

Now Kate Murray says that Maureen was in the scullery with Mary Cole, 'I was in the kitchen. Mary Cole came into the kitchen with the kettle and she sent Maureen back with it. Maureen then went out. It was the last time I saw her alive. That was when Mary Cole was making the feeding for the calf. Shortly after Mary Cole left the scullery, I saw her go out. I didn't see where she went. I didn't see Maureen go out of the house. I missed Maureen a few minutes after Mary Cole had gone out. I went out and searched and I couldn't find her. I heard Mary Cole calling to the children outside. I asked her if Maureen was with her and she said 'No.' That was about 20 minutes after she had gone out. On the evening Maureen was drowned, Mary Cole said she couldn't see the cow at first and she went up by Father Walsh's ditch and found the cattle at the other side of the river amongst the furze. She said that to me when I asked her where she got the cattle. There was no one else there at the time' and further on she said, 'I made a remark to Mary Cole how was it she couldn't see the child and she only a short distance before her and she said she didn't see her.'

Now Mary Cole's account of her movements on that evening is as follows. She says: 'On the 22nd of August I was employed at Flynn's. I was doing the ordinary work. In the evening I was in my bedroom about 5 o'clock. Maureen came in. I started doing some things. I started preparing the food for the calf. There was nobody with me but Maureen. Maureen went and took back the kettle to the kitchen. After that I remember her going in through the kitchen towards the front door. I didn't know which way she went.'

I think Tynan supplies the answer to that. Mary Cole said she went out a few minutes afterwards and according to Tynan's evidence, Maureen was on the road a short distance in front of her. Mary Cole continues and says, 'Kate Murray was sitting at the fire with a book in her hand. In about 5 minutes I went out for the cow. I went out the back door. I had a bucket in my hand which was used for feeding the calf. I went out the front of the house and out the front gate. I saw Jack Tynan on the bicycle and he spoke to me. I passed by the school.'

That is the place where Maureen is alleged to have passed a few minutes before. 'I fed the calf' she says. 'It was a few yards from the gate. There was some cattle there. I remained with the calf while it fed for about 7 or 8 minutes and I then turned home the cow.' Then she says, 'I was with the calf about 4 or 5 yards from the gate. I do not recollect telling Mr. Flynn that I found the cow among the furze' and then she deals with the statement she made to the police as regards where she found the cow and she said she never told a different story to anyone else, and that when she made the statement she had no reason to believe that she would be arrested.

Now, that is the whole of the evidence in the case. The last portion of Mary Cole's evidence is, 'When I made the statements I had no reason to believe I would be arrested,' and Mr. Walsh made comment to you to similar effect. He said she had no idea when she made the statement that she was going to be arrested and Mr. Walsh then asks you, 'Why then should she not tell the truth?' If, of course, she was an innocent girl that had nothing to do with the drowning of these two children, that would be a most pertinent question, but if she were a girl who had in fact drowned the children then there is a pretty obvious reason why she should not tell the truth whether she suspected she was going to be arrested or not.

Mr. Walsh has also referred you to the effect of an adverse verdict against this girl. He says it would mean separating her from her mother and that the separation of a mother from her daughter is worse and more sorrowful than death.

Gentlemen, that is not really a matter for you. It is a matter of some consolation in this case that whatever may be your verdict the accused on account of her age is not subject to the death sentence. That is a matter of some consolation but you must not pay undue weight to that either in favour of or against the accused.

You have to try questions of fact and you must try and determine these questions to the best of your ability on the evidence before you and not take into consideration the consequences of your verdict to the accused or any body else. That is what you have sworn to do.

You will deal with the two cases separately. First, you will deal with the case of Philomena, and in her case, as in the case of Maureen, there are two questions on the evidence in this case which you will have to determine. First was the drowning accidental and if it was not accidental was it caused by the accused?

The same two questions will arise in connection with the death of Maureen. Now, glancing for a moment at the case against the accused in respect of the death of Philomena, we see these salient facts. The child is a child of one year and ten months old and the entire of this fence with the exception of the one spot where the tree stump is, the entire of that fence from the point (indicated) opposite the school wall to Longford Cross is a high fence with bushes growing on the top to a height in places of in or about 7 or 8 feet.

When the police officers went there some months afterwards, they found a gap in the fence. At the time of the occurrence, that gap was filled up as you would naturally expect in the case of a gap leading to a field of oats at its full height. The gap at that time, according to the evidence, was filled up and according to Mr. Flynn, it was impossible for a fowl to get in there.

You go down along and at the bridge there is some kind of what one witness referred to as a rough stile. There are no steps in the ordinary sense and the only way to get across the fence in that portion, which is as high as the remainder of the fence, is by getting hold of portion of the tree and swinging yourself across and this I suggest to you would be beyond the powers of a child of this age.

You come to the old tree stump. At this place according to the evidence, the fence on the road side is from two and a half to three feet high and on the inside there is a depth of five feet or so and even in that case I think you will have difficulty in coming to the conclusion that a child of these tender years would have been capable of getting across there.

I think such a thing would hardly have been suggested to you at all but for the incident of the 15th of July; and when you are dealing with that incident as you must in leading up to the occurrence of the 27th of July you have the evidence of Mary Cole on the one hand and Brophy on the other hand and the evidence of the two witnesses is not in agreement as it seems to me.

The evidence of Brophy is that the child was standing inside the fence, crying. He got off his bicycle, spoke to it and pacified it and remained with it until Mary Cole came up and he called her and told her to take it away.

That is not the appearance as it seems to me of a child that was wandering away. It rather presents the appearance of a child that was brought down and left there while the person with it went away, probably for an innocent purpose, possibly for some other purpose.

At any rate, shortly afterwards, according to Brophy, Mary Cole came up and he sent the child home. Were it not for that incident, it would not be suggested here that this child was capable of going down and getting into the field. You must make up your mind about it and about the two witnesses and if you come to the conclusion that you can place very little reliance on Mary Cole's account of that incident— if you come to the conclusion that you don't think the child strayed down there itself on that evening, but rather that it was brought down and left there, then of course that would cause you to approach the drowning of the child on the 27th of July from a somewhat different point of view.

Do you believe that this child was capable of going down there and getting into that field at any point and going and getting into the river at the point where it was found?

Apart from the place at the tree-stump there is scarcely any other place where it could have got in. The gate at Longford Cross is fastened. There is netting on it up to a height and the child could not get in unless it climbed the gate.

Mrs. Flynn went down and examined the gate and the gate was closed and fastened. It is a gate that does not swing easily. You have to lift it to open it. The child is found down here at this point where the river is four yards wide. It is within three feet of the right hand bank and the evidence of Gorman who found the child is that in his opinion, it must have got in from the right bank.

If you take the view that it was from the right bank it got in, do you think there was any possibility whatever of its crossing this fence across which according to Mr. Flynn, scarcely a fowl could pass, then working its way through the oat-field, over the barbed wire and getting down to that point and falling in?

On the other hand, if you think there is a possibility that it got down in this direction and wandered along this long rough field with all the obstacles, which you heard of in the evidence, and some of which you saw in the photographs, and finally got down to this point and into the river—got some distance across and got into the position where it was found drowned three feet from the right hand bank, then, of course, that would be an accident, but if you exclude that and come to the conclusion that this child was brought there and drowned then, by whom was it done? By whom was it brought there?

It is not suggested that there is any other person with such ill-will against the Flynns that he or she could or would be capable of committing this crime.

There is evidence—evidence which appears to me to be trustworthy but, as I told you at the commencement of the case, such questions are for you and not for me—but there is evidence which appears to me trustworthy that at a particular time that afternoon, shortly before this child was found drowned, Mary Cole was seen in the field with a child dressed in a red cloak, a child of scarcely two years and that some ten or fifteen minutes afterwards she was seen again in the field but that time there was no child seen with her. Where was the child at that time? Remember the evidence of Delaney, that the three older children had gone up the road in the other direction and Philomena was not with them. Where was she? Had she gone down to the field with Mary Cole? And, was she in the field with Mary Cole at the time Hennessy passed by?

If you come to the conclusion that she was, then where was she at the time Mary Bostick passed down? A few minutes afterwards she was drowned. A case might have been made by the accused that she went to this field this evening, that she brought the child with her, that she forgot her there, came back with the cow and left her behind, forgot all about her. But that is not the case that is made. Her case is, that she was not in the field at all, that she found the cattle in the field on the other side of the road, and drove them across the river, drove them out at the school gate.

With reference to these matters, you must decide between the evidence of Mary Cole on the one hand, and Hennessy and Mary Bostick on the other, and determine which of them you will believe. And dealing with the evidence of any witness you will, as I would suggest to you, apply this test: if you are satisfied that any particular witness is telling an untruth, a thing that to the knowledge of that witness must be untrue, in one respect, you will probably place very little reliance on that witness in other respects, because a person that tells a lie on oath on one matter won't have much difficulty in repeating it in respect of another matter.

A red coat is found in the house the following Monday. Was it the red coat which Hennessy saw in the field and was it the red coat which was produced here? If so, how did it get back to the house? If the case for the prosecution is right that Mary Cole is responsible for the drowning of the child, there is an obvious way in which it could come back and if that cause is right, there is an obvious reason why it should be brought back to suggest that the child wandered alone and was not dressed for out of doors at the time it went away. If it was the same red coat, how did it get back to the house save through the instrumentality of the accused, Mary Cole?

We come to the drowning of Maureen and the issues there are the same issues as in the case of Philomena but the circumstances are very different. Maureen was found drowned in eight or nine inches of water, eight or nine inches at the most. The greater portion of the body was out of the water. The back of the head was out of the water.

The face was down in the water and there is a mark caused by external violence on her forehead.

It is hardly conceivable that this little girl, almost seven years of age, went out and got drowned accidentally. It is almost impossible. The only possible explanation of such a thing, as it seems to me, is that the child had fallen and stunned herself and lain there. She went up there, and Mary Cole was undoubtedly in that field on her own evidence, and that is a matter you must consider. If you come to the conclusion that Maureen was not drowned accidentally but as the result of her face being held under the water until she was unconscious.

If you come to that conclusion, who was responsible? The little girl was alive about 5:30. Shortly after that time she left the kitchen, went out and certainly went up to the spot at which she was subsequently found drowned. Tynan says that he was coming down the road and he saw her in front of the school. A few minutes afterwards, perhaps seconds rather than minutes, when he got to Flynn's gate, the child had disappeared, presumably into the gate leading into the field. Mary Cole was coming out and that she was in the field is beyond all questions—she says so herself. Here again there is a discrepancy in her evidence, in the statement she gave to the police and in the statement she gave to Mr. Flynn and Kate Murray after the occurrence.

She says she got the cow and the calf in just inside the gate— within four or five yards of the gate and was never up the field at all. Mr. Flynn tells you, she told him, she got them up here (indicated). He asked her was it amongst the furze and she said, 'Yes', and the place he knew where the furze were, was in the triangular corner, past the place where Maureen was drowned.

Kate Murray didn't know the place and for that reason you will probably consider that her evidence in that respect is entitled to all the more weight because she says Mary Cole gave her an account where she went for the cows and she says she went up by the priest's field and got the cow, up in the far corner and what is still more remarkable and what puts the possibility of a mistake, to my mind, is out of the question, she said, according to her evidence she said to Mary Cole, 'how was it you didn't see the child and she such a short distance in front?'

Mary Cole says she never went up there at all. Do you accept her evidence in that respect or do you rather accept as true what she said to Mr. Flynn and to Kate Murray, according to their evidence that she had gone up and got the cow—up in this direction (indicated)—that she had been up near the place, past the place where Maureen was found drowned?

If you come to that conclusion, if you come to the conclusion, first that the death was not accidental and was brought about by human agency you will ask yourselves by whose agency? Was it by the agency of the girl who, according to some evidence, according to her own statements, passed in or about the place at or about the time at which Maureen must have been drowned?

Now these are all the remarks I have to address to you in reference to these occurrences. As I told you at the commencement of the case and I now repeat, the accused is entitled to the benefit of any reasonable doubt which you may have on either or any of these issues. I have already explained to you what a reasonable doubt is. It is a doubt which reasonable men of the world recognise and act upon in their own important affairs of life. If in reference to any of these issues which you have to try, you have such a doubt as that you will give the prisoner the benefit of it. If there is no such doubt in our mind, if you are satisfied beyond any such doubt as that the accused is guilty on one or more of these charges you will so find."

The Jury retired to consider its verdict at 4:30 p.m., and then Mr. Walsh asked, "I respectfully ask your Lordship to tell the Jury that it is common case that Mary Cole went down the field, at the end of the schoolhouse, on the evening of the 22nd August with a bucket and that there is abundant evidence, that the bucket contained food for the calf."

Mr. Justice O'Byrne: "You are not suggesting that I suggested anything else to the Jury?"

Mr. Walsh: "With great respect, not at all, but your Lordship's Charge to the Jury, I respectfully submit, may be open to the inference that there was a dispute about the bucket. I ask you to tell the Jury, as a matter of Law, that before they can convict upon circumstantial evidence, not only must the circumstances relied upon be consistent of guilt of the prisoner, but there must be at least one circumstance, inconsistent with any other conclusion than that."

Mr. Justice O'Byrne: "Do you think I have left the Jury in any doubt about all such matters?"

Mr. Walsh: "If your Lordship pleases?"

Mr. Justice O'Byrne: "No, I don't think it is necessary to recall the Jury for either of these."

CHAPTER TWENTY-ONE

MRS. FLYNN IS CALLED BEFORE MR. JUSTICE O'BYRNE

❧

Aunt Kit Fogarty came to Dublin for the trial and attended court every day with Mammy and Daddy as their support.

She played no other part in the proceedings and very likely guided Statia in dressing and courtroom etiquette. The Prosecuting team of William Carrigan K.C. and Dudley White K.C., very likely during their interviews before she gave her evidence would go over the questions that she would be asked and would instruct her to answer questions put to her by the State and the Defence (Mr. James J. Walsh), in a 'yes' or 'no' manner and not to go into more detail until asked. The same advice would have been given to Daddy.

After sitting through the addresses by Mr. Walsh K.C. and Mr. Carrigan K.C. Statia endured the detailed Judge's Instructions to the Jury.

Mr. Walsh told the Jury that: 'While my sympathies go out to every father and mother who lose their children in any circumstances, and especially in these circumstances, where two little girls were brought in dead from the river, very little of my sympathy goes out to Mrs. Flynn. He justified this statement by suggesting that the Flynns were privileged people, who were in receipt of £550 a year as National Teachers; they had, in addition, a farm of thirty acres and stock. They also had a motor car. These are the poor people, according to Mr. Carrigan, who can afford only one servant, Mary Cole, who was the absolute slave in this household'. (He neglected to mention the financial cost of rearing five children and the difficulty of holding down a job as a school teacher at the same time plus the advantages to Mary Cole of her first employed position with the school Master and Mistress.

Later in his address to the jury he added: 'While sorrow had come into the home of Mr. and Mrs. Flynn when their children were taken from them, the parting of a mother with her convict daughter, her first child, was a greater sorrow'.

Is it any wonder then, why, after the Jury were ordered by the Judge to retire to consider their verdict, when Michael and Statia and Kit Fogarty were in the lobby outside the Courtroom, Statia, against the advice of her sister, went up to Mr. Walsh who was standing there with his associate, Mr. Lavery, and she expressed her fury after his remarks: "Go on, you pup. Your mother would not be proud of you today".

Granted that she might be forgiven for not saving her anger for later after the verdict, she was the mother that we all knew as we grew up and when we failed to toe the line she would 'tear a strip' off the offender. And her students would also be subject to her anger. As a mother she practiced 'tough love' long before that phrase was invented.

Mr. Walsh complained to His Lordship who brought Statia before the bench and told her:

"An incident of a very unpleasant nature has been mentioned to me. It appears that during the interval you met Counsel for the Defence outside this court and made an observation to him which he reported to me.

I have taken into account the very natural strain under which you must be laboring, and on account of that I pass over the incident. Were it not for that, I would have taken a very drastic course."

CHAPTER TWENTY-TWO

THE VERDICT

ॐ

The jury was absent for forty minutes and with great solemnity they filed back into the Court.

The verdict was read to the hushed courtroom.

"Guilty" on both accounts.

The girl in the dock, who had been carefully watching the jurymen as they filed into their places, displayed not the slightest sign of emotion when the result of their deliberations was announced.

His Lordship, Mr. Justice O'Byrne addressing her, said:

"Mary Cole, you have been convicted after a long and careful trial, of the murder of two little children, one of them under two years and the other under seven. The murder of children of that age is, under any circumstances, so utterly abhorrent to every natural instinct that it is difficult to imagine how such a crime could be committed. But it is all the more abhorrent when, as in this case, the children who were murdered were children to whom, for a period of in or about a year, you had been attending day after day, seeing after their wants, nursing them, feeding them and caring for them.

If you had been a few months older, these crimes would have entailed a sentence of death. By reason of your age, the law has mercifully enacted that you will not suffer such a sentence, and I will now pronounce that sentence which the law prescribes for such offence—that you will be detained during the pleasure of His Excellency the Governor General."

The prisoner turned round sharply to the place close by where her mother was in tears, and was then conducted by the wardress from the dock without showing any sign of feeling.

When the accused had been found guilty and sentenced, Mr. Walsh asked, "Will your Lordship grant me Certificate for Leave to Appeal?"

Mr. Justice O'Byrne: "On what grounds?"

Mr. Walsh: "On the ground that I stated to your Lordship when the Jury retired, viz.—that your Lordship should direct the jury, that before they convict upon circumstantial evidence, not only must there be consistent with guilt of the prisoner but that there must be at least one Circumstance, inconsistent with any other Conclusion than Guilt, and on the ground my Lord, that your Lordship directed the Jury, that there was no evidence of any ill will against the Flynns by any other people, and third, my submission is, the ground that your Lordship did not stress to the Jury the evidence given by the accused herself, and in her Statement to the same degree as the evidence for the State."

Mr. Justice O'Byrne: "I refuse the Application Mr. Walsh."

INDICTMENT AND VERDICT
DATED MARCH 23, 1928

— source: *Trial File Document 1928*

NOTICE OF APPLICATION FOR LEAVE TO APPEAL
DATED MARCH 27, 1928

— source: *Trial File Document 1928*

CHAPTER TWENTY-THREE

THE APPEAL

❧

On March 24, 1928, Mary Cole was sent to Mountjoy Female Prison in Dublin. On March 27th she signed an application for legal aid and for a copy of the transcript of the evidence to be provided to her free of charge for the purpose of appealing her conviction.

GROUNDS FOR APPLICATION

1. (a) Non-direction amounting to misdirection in as much as the purport of the learned Trial Judge's charge was to invite the opinion of the Jury as to whether or not the facts were consistent with the prisoner's guilt. It is submitted that the proper direction would have been to have further asked the Jury to consider whether the facts were inconsistent with any other rational conclusion and further the Learned Judge omitted to direct the Jury that is was only in the event of their finding the facts inconsistent with any other conclusion than that of guilt that they could safely convict the accused.

   (b) Was wrong on a point of law in declining to accede to the request by Counsel to direct the Jury as in paragraph (a) hereof.

2. Misdirection on a point of law in reference to sentence particulars whereof are set out in paragraph 6(b) hereof.

3. Misdirection or non-direction amounting to a misdirection on a point of law. The Learned Judge in commenting on the evidence of the Prisoner referred to certain discrepancies in her evidence in comparison with some of the evidence for the prosecution and thereupon proceeded to tell the jury that if they found her evidence false in one detail they were at liberty to reject the entire of her evidence. The Learned Trial Judge omitted to direct the Jury that although the prisoner had given evidence, the onus of

proof was never upon her at any stage of the proceedings and that the Statute entitling the prisoner to give evidence had not altered the Law regarding the *onus probandi* in a criminal case. The Jury under these circumstances was left to conclude that if they could not accept the entire of the prisoner's evidence, they could convict her.

4. The verdict cannot reasonably be sustained upon the evidence, proper to have been considered by the Jury.

5. The verdict was against evidence and the weight of evidence.

6. That the Trial was unsatisfactory:

(a) In that the facts were (in disregard of the evidence) grossly exaggerated by the Counsel for the prosecution, who described the prisoner as a person of a certain mental type meaning thereby of a class of person, naturally liable to commit a crime of this nature on account of her mental condition. There was no evidence, whatever tendered, to support this statement which prejudicially to the prisoner affected the minds of the Jurors.

(b) Counsel for the prosecution was permitted to tell the Jury, notwithstanding objection by Counsel for the Prisoner, that the Prisoner was not liable to the sentence of death in the event of the Prisoner being found guilty of murder. This statement was irrelevant to any question proper for determination by the Jury, it was purely a legal consequence of their verdict and it was misdirection in point of law to allow the Jury to take it into consideration at all. This misdirection lessened the sense of responsibility of the Jurors in arriving at their verdict.

(c) The Learned Trial Judge omitted in connection with defence of accident to draw the attention of the Jury in the course of his charge, to the evidence of Mr. Flynn, one of the witnesses for the prosecution, that the body of the child Maureen was found at a crossing place in the river.

(d) The Learned Trial Judge omitted to tell the Jury that the evidence of Mrs. Flynn in reference to the red coat would tend to bear out the evidence given by the Prisoner rather than that of

John Hennessey, that the child Philomena was not wearing the red coat.

(e) The evidence of John Gorman that the prisoner used the words "Wouldn't it be awful if she was drowned?" was placed before the Jury apart from the context in such a way as to indicate only an adverse meaning.

Signed: Mary Cole

Witness: John J. Hannan, Solicitor
            205 Pearse St., Dublin
Date: 27th day of March, 1928

DISMISSAL OF APPEAL

<u>Memorandum:</u>

May 24, 1928

From: The Governor, Mountjoy Prison,
To: The Registrar, Criminal Appeal Courts, Dublin Castle

A Chara:

I beg to acknowledge receipt of Order of the Court of Criminal Appeal, dismissing the Appeal of Mary Cole, and to inform you that the enclosure was duly handed to her.

Mise, le meas

Sean O'Cománaig
Governor

—   *source: Trial File Document 1928*

On August, 28, 1928, the following petition was submitted to the President of the Executive Council, (Taoiseach—W.T. Cosgrave).

Mr. Banim (Secretary to the President) wrote:

"The Minister for Justice has requested me to lay before the President the position as regards Mary Cole who was convicted of the murder of two children at the Central Criminal Court on 23rd March last. Will you please take steps to bring this minute to the attention of the President when a suitable opportunity presents itself at the conclusion of all the functions and ceremonies in which the President is at present immersed?

Although Mary Cole was found guilty of murder she was not liable to the death penalty. Section 103 of the Children Act, 1908, enacts that when a person under 16 years of age is convicted of murder such person shall be detained during the pleasure of the Governor General in lieu of being sentenced to death and when sentenced such person is liable to be detained in such place and under such conditions as the Minister for Justice may direct and whilst so detained shall be deemed to be in legal custody. As a temporary measure the Minister for Justice made an order on the 24th of March last, directing that Mary Cole should be detained in Mountjoy Female Prison and that until she should attain the age of 21 years she should be subject to the rules with respect to prisoners between the ages of 16 and 21 years. Whilst no other reasonable course appears to have been possible the Minister for Justice has never been quite satisfied as to the treatment to which Mary Cole should be subjected. In the present month he was approached by Miss Kathleen Sullivan, one of the [two recently appointed and only] Probation Officers attached to the District Court who is interested in Mary Cole's case and was concerned to suggest some treatment which might be more calculated to transform this wretched girl than detention in Mountjoy Female Prison. Miss Sullivan represented that Sister Superior of the Sisters of Charity of St. Vincent De Paul,

9 and 10 Henrietta Street, Dublin, was prepared to take Mary Cole under her care. The Minister has now issued a licence under Section 10b of the Children Act, 1908, permitting Mary Cole to be discharged from Mountjoy Female Prison to the care of the Sister Superior's authority. I enclose herewith a copy of the licence. If Mary Cole leaves Henrietta Street she can be, and will be, sent back again to Prison.

The Minister for Justice is satisfied that this is a satisfactory solution of the difficulty presented by Mary Cole's case and he would like the President to know what exactly has been done for her. She will be under proper reformative influences and at the same time the community will be protected from a person of the gravest criminal tendencies. If she, after a space of years, appears to be completely reformed the question of allowing her at large can be considered. If the Nuns fail to keep control over her, we can always send her back to Prison.

(signed)
RUNAIDHE
(Initialed) "I approve" J.T. McC.

≈

Order by the Minister of Justice to transfer Mary Cole from Mountjoy Prison to the Sisters of Charity:

SAORSTÁT ÉIREANN

In pursuance of the powers vested in me by Section 10b of the Children Act, 1908, as adopted by the Children Act, 1908, Adoption Order, 1928, and of every and any other power me in this behalf enabling, I, JAMES FITZGERALD-KENNEY, Minister for Justice, do by this Licence permit Mary Cole who, at the Central Criminal Court held at Dublin on the 23rd day of March, 1928, was convicted of murder, and being a person under the age of sixteen years, was ordered to be detained during the pleasure of His Excellency, the Governor General, and is now detained in Mountjoy Female Prison, to be discharged from the said Prison within thirty days from the date hereof on condition that she places herself and remains during the continuance of this licence under the care, supervision and authority of the Sister Superior for the time being of the Sisters of Charity of Saint Vincent de Paul, 9 and 10 Henrietta Street, Dublin.

Given under my hand and seal
this 28th day of August, 1928.

JAMES FITZGERALD-KENNEY
MINISTER FOR JUSTICE

On 6th September, 1928 a memorandum from the Cabinet was addressed to Mr. O'Friel, Secretary, Department of Justice:

"I have shown the President your minute of 28th August regarding the case of Mary Cole. The President is very pleased with the steps taken and appreciates the manner in which the matter has been dealt with."

— *source: Trial File Document 1928*

EPILOGUE

MARY COLE

~

"Detained during the pleasure of His Excellency The Governor General". This was the sentence handed down by Justice O'Byrne to Mary Cole. Prior to 1921 the wording would have been "detained at His Majesty's pleasure". The Irish Free State inherited the English justice system and the English Monarch appointed the Governor General as his representative in Ireland. This ended when the Irish Republic was declared in 1949.

This sentence was often used in the case of juvenile offenders as a substitute for life sentencing. It would apply to Mary Cole. This sentence would be subject to review and would be deemed to be complete where the reviewing body is satisfied that there has been a significant change in the offender's attitude and behaviour.

Therefore, it is likely that Mary Cole's sentence would have been served 'Under License' under the rules of the Sisters of Charity to whose care she was transferred from Mountjoy Female Prison following the intervention of the Probation Officer, Miss Kathleen Sullivan in August 1928.

It is very likely that she would have been approved for release at age 21 if not earlier.

THE FLYNN FAMILY

❧

Michael and Statia Flynn moved from Camross with their three remaining children, Eilis, Patricia and Michael to Tipperary in 1927, prior to the Garda investigation and before Mary was charged. As is usual with teachers transferring from one school to another, this is planned to commence at the new school at the beginning of the academic year, September.

I have no information as to how this took place considering the disposal and/or sale of their cows, arranging the physical transportation of their household belongings, acceptance at the Tipperary and Ballyhurst National Schools.

Statia was able to go on a pilgrimage to Lourdes prior to starting her new position and she rarely missed attending daily Mass. Since the National Schools were at that time managed by the Parish Priests, one can assume that there were vacancies, and interviews to be completed in a short space of time.

On July 27th, Philomena was found drowned.

On August 22nd, Maureen was found drowned.

And on August 25th, the first fire was discovered.

On August 31, 1927, the second fire was found the day Mary's employment with the Flynns came to the end of her notice. At that time there was no suspicion of foul play. In fact, she was given a present by Statia on her departure.

The Gardaí commenced their investigation in September and continued until she was formally charged on November 16, 1927. Then she appeared before the District Justice on December 9th.

Michael and Statia settled in Tipperary with their three remaining children and Katie Tobin and Katherine Murray before suspicion was aroused.

They took up residence in the house beside the National School in Tipperary, where Sean was born in January 1928. Statia had commenced as Principal at Ballyhurst about three miles outside Tipperary and Michael drove her there every morning and picked her up after school every day until she was appointed to the Girls'

National School in Tipperary some years later. Sometimes, weather permitting, she would ride her bicycle to Ballyhurst. Her pupils, all from farming families, would often bring donations of sods of turf, blocks of wood or eggs to the school.

In the early 1930s a world depression was having an effect on the Irish economy and especially on large families. Unemployment in Ireland forced many fathers to move to England in order to support those at home.

Aunt Kit came from London to visit over the holidays. Sean was born in the local nursing home on January 2, 1928, the first of seven more boys, so their new location over the Christmas and New Year must have been the scene of much emotional pain and distress.

The children born in Tipperary grew up without knowledge of the events in Camross, other than misinformation whispered but not a subject to be discussed. It is not unusual for life to continue in Irish families without disclosure of tragic events of the past.

The story of the tragic drownings has been reported over recent years by a number of writers, sometimes with inaccuracies. This account by a family member was prompted to correct relevant misinformation for the benefit of this generation, based on factual trial evidence and corroboration from newspaper accounts of the trial, as well as information collected from reliable sources.

Statia was an active contributor to the National Folklore Commission. Stories, folklore, piseógs, poetry and songs were submitted by adults and children from small rural communities all over the country and were published by University College Dublin.

Michael became active in an organisation called *Muintir Na Tíre*, People of the Land, founded in 1931 by a Tipperary priest, Fr. Hayes. This became an aggressive, active, non-political movement which was dedicated to improving the social, cultural, economic and environmental status of rural communities all over Ireland. Parish guilds were set up, each responsible for setting priorities. Such priorities as public water supply, rural electrification, local industrial development and tourism were the most common projects undertaken without government interference and sometimes without episcopal approval. Michael served as Joint Treasurer of the organisation for many years.

Meanwhile their children were always supervised and encouraged to achieve a first class primary and secondary education which led each one to a profession. Their direction was all the more remarkable when considering the impact of World War II, Ireland's struggle to establish itself as a new nation and the formation of the League of Nations which later became the United Nations Organisation.

The students of Michael and Statia frequently returned after graduating to successful careers to express their thanks for the sound educational foundation under their tutelage.

Mammy and Daddy (with family dog Pal) c. 1953
— *credit: Author's Collection*

PRAYER CARD FOR
PHILOMENA AND MAUREEN FLYNN

In Loving Memory
— OF —

PHILOMENA FLYNN

CAMROSS,

WHO DIED

On 27th July, 1927,

AGED 1 YEAR, 10 MONTHS.

AND OF

MAUREEN FLYNN

CAMROSS,

WHO DIED

On 22nd August, 1927,

AGED 6 YEARS, 10 MONTHS.

"THY WILL BE DONE."

— credit: Author's Collection

Philomena Flynn
died on July 27, 1927

Maureen Flynn
died on August 22, 1927

Michael Joseph Flynn
died on September 25, 1963

Eilis McCarthy (nee Flynn)
died on March 4, 1974

Colm Flynn
died on January 11, 1976

Statia Flynn
died on April 6, 1978

Father Sean Flynn
died on July 8, 1978

Father Michael Flynn
died on January 1, 1995

Father Patrick Flynn
died on April 24, 2007

Patricia Upton (nee Flynn)
died on July 1, 2008

Brendan Flynn
died February 15, 2010

Ailbe Flynn
died on September 29, 2012

May They Rest in Peace

The Flynn Family c. 1953

Back row: Colm, Eilis, Kevin, Father Sean (insert) Brendan, Patty, Kieran
Middle row: Father Paddy, Statia, Michael, Father Michael
Front row: Ailbe

— *source: Author's Collection*

THE LITTLE RED COAT

INDEX

❧

Dowling, Pat, details influence of Michael
J. Flynn on education, 37

Dwyer, Mr. William, Solicitor, instructed
the Defence, 79

F

Flynn, Ailbe (brother), *Consecration*
certificate, 32, born, 38

Flynn, Ailbe (son), tape recorder gift, 16,
commemoration and scholarship at his
Law school, 5

Flynn, Anastatia (Statia), dedication, 9,
attendance log Maureen's name struck off,
25, 26, *Consecration* certificate, 31, born in
Killoran, Moyne, siblings 37, parlour
meeting with Fr. Walsh, 41, searches for
Maureen, 51, identifies red coat under
cross-examination, 87, recalled to answer
Jury's questions, 119, denies giving the red
coat to Mary to have washed, 119

Flynn, Brendan, *Consecration* certificate, 32,
born, 38

Flynn, Colm (Columba), *Consecration*
certificate, 32, born, 38

Flynn, Eilis (Lizzie, Elizabeth), *Consecration*
certificate, 31, born, 38, mentioned in
Mary's second statement, 68

Flynn, Father Michael, missionary in The
Gambia, 24, *Consecration* certificate, 31,
born, 38

Flynn, Father Patrick (Paddy), *Consecration*
certificate, 32, born, 38

Flynn, Father Sean, *Consecration*
certificate, 32, born, 38, 181, Statia
pregnant with, 57

Flynn, Kevin (Author), Foreword,
Consecration certificate, 32, born, 38,
commemoration of family, 185

Flynn, Kieran T., discovery of events, 11,
Consecration certificate, 32, born, 38

Flynn, Maureen (Mary), born, 38,
Consecration certificate, 31, name struck off
roll book, 26, is last seen alive, 51, is
discovered drowned, 53

Flynn, Michael J., dedication, 9,
Consecration certificate, 31, born and
education, 36, educated at De La Salle
College in Waterford, siblings, 36, farming
income, 40, returns home to learn
Philomena is dead, 47, looks for Maureen,
51, gives evidence at trial, 80, cross-
examination begins, 95, testifies where he
found Maureen, 96

Flynn, Patricia (Patty), *Consecration*
certificate, 31, born, 38

Flynn, Patrick (of Rathdowney), father of
Michael J. Flynn, 22

Flynn, Philomena (Phil), born, 38, Statia
never sees her alive again, 45, is discovered
drowned, 47

Fogarty (Matron), Katherine (Aunt Kit),
life history, awarded M.B.E. in 1961, 81,
died 1996, 83, newspaper clippings of
indictment, 29, arrives from London to
lend support to Statia, 80, attends Court
each day to support Statia and Michael,
165

G

Gardaí (Garda), credit for investigation, 15,
continue inquiries after Maureen's inquest,
57

Gleeson, Joe & Kate Gleeson in Mary's
second statement, 72

Gorman, John, joins the search for
Philomena, 46, picks up Philomena's body,
47, mentioned in Mary's first statement,
76, testifies at trial, 99

H

Healy, Father, Statia asks to join the search
for Philomena, 46

THE LITTLE RED COAT

10313048R00104

Printed in Great Britain
by Amazon